CONTEMPORARY WRITERS

General Editors
MALCOLM BRADBURY
and
CHRISTOPHER BIGSBY

JOHN BARTH

IN THE SAME SERIES

Donald Barthelme   *M. Couturier and R. Durand*
Saul Bellow   *Malcolm Bradbury*
Richard Brautigan   *Marc Chénetier*
E. L. Doctorow   *Paul Levine*
Margaret Drabble   *Joanne V. Creighton*
J. G. Farrell   *Ronald Binns*
John Fowles   *Peter Conradi*
Günter Grass   *Ronald Hayman*
Graham Greene   *John Spurling*
Seamus Heaney   *Blake Morrison*
Ted Hughes   *Thomas West*
Philip Larkin   *Andrew Motion*
John le Carré   *Eric Homberger*
Doris Lessing   *Lorna Sage*
Malcolm Lowry   *Ronald Binns*
David Mamet   *C. W. E. Bigsby*
Iris Murdoch   *Richard Todd*
Joe Orton   *C. W. E. Bigsby*
Harold Pinter   *G. Almansi and S. Henderson*
Thomas Pynchon   *Tony Tanner*
Alain Robbe-Grillet   *John Fletcher*
Philip Roth   *Hermione Lee*
Muriel Spark   *Alan Bold*
Kurt Vonnegut   *Jerome Klinkowitz*
Patrick White   *John Colmer*

JOHN
BARTH

HEIDE ZIEGLER

METHUEN
LONDON AND NEW YORK

First published in 1987 by
Methuen & Co. Ltd
11 New Fetter Lane, London EC4P 4EE

Published in the USA by
Methuen & Co.
in association with Methuen, Inc.
29 West 35th Street, New York, NY 10001

Typeset by Rowland Phototypesetting Ltd
Printed in Great Britain by
Biddles Ltd, Guildford and King's Lynn

British Library Cataloguing in Publication Data
Ziegler, Heide
John Barth. – (Contemporary writers)
1. Barth, John – Criticism and interpretation
I. Title   II. Series
813'.54   PS3552.A75

ISBN 0-416-34700-2

Library of Congress Cataloging in Publication Data
Ziegler, Heide.
John Barth.

(Contemporary writers)
Bibliography: p.
1. Barth, John – Criticism and interpretation.
I. Title.   II. Series
PS3552.A75Z97 1987   813'.54   86-32427
ISBN 0-416-34700-2 (pbk)

For the Author

CONTENTS

General editors' preface 8

Acknowledgments 10

A note on the texts 11

1 Introduction: The sense of an ending 12

2 The supra-existentialist novel:
The Floating Opera and *The End of the Road* 19

3 The supra-*Bildungsroman*:
The Sot-Weed Factor and *Giles Goat-Boy* 31

4 The supra-*Künstlerroman*:
Lost in the Funhouse and *Chimera* 49

5 The supra-realistic novel:
LETTERS and *Sabbatical* 64

6 Conclusion: The sense of a beginning 84

Notes 90

Bibliography 93

GENERAL EDITORS' PREFACE

The contemporary is a country which we all inhabit, but there is little agreement as to its boundaries or its shape. The serious writer is one of its most sensitive interpreters, but criticism is notoriously cautious in offering a response or making a judgement. Accordingly, this continuing series is an endeavour to look at some of the most important writers of our time, and the questions raised by their work. It is, in effect, an attempt to map the contemporary, to describe its aesthetic and moral topography.

The series came into existence out of two convictions. One was that, despite all the modern pressures on the writer and on literary culture, we live in a major creative time, as vigorous and alive in its distinctive way as any that went before. The other was that, though criticism itself tends to grow more theoretical and apparently indifferent to contemporary creation, there are grounds for a lively aesthetic debate. This series, which includes books written from various standpoints, is meant to provide a forum for that debate. By design, some of those who have contributed are themselves writers, willing to respond to their contemporaries; others are critics who have brought to the discussion of current writing the spirit of contemporary criticism or simply a conviction, forcibly and coherently argued, for the contemporary significance of their subjects. Our aim, as the series develops, is to continue to explore the works of major post-war writers – in fiction, drama and poetry – over an international range, and thereby to illuminate not only those works but also in some degree the artistic, social and moral assumptions on which they rest. Our wish is that, in their very variety of approach and emphasis, these books will stimulate interest in and understanding of the vitality of a living literature which, because it is contemporary, is especially ours.

Norwich, England

MALCOLM BRADBURY
CHRISTOPHER BIGSBY

ACKNOWLEDGMENTS

I am indebted to the editor of *The International Fiction Review* for permission to reprint, in modified form, my review of John Barth's novel *Sabbatical*.

For help in typing and revising the manuscript, Barbara Heidinger, Patrick O'Donnell, and particularly Thomas J. Minnes have my gratitude. I also wish to thank Christopher Bigsby and Malcolm Bradbury for trust, support, and critical suggestions.

Finally, I thank John Barth for his continuing interest in my continuing interest in his work.

The author and publisher would like to thank the following for permission to quote copyright material: Bantam Books for extracts from *The Floating Opera, The End of the Road, The Sot-Weed Factor* and *Lost in the Funhouse*; Doubleday & Co. Inc. for extracts from *Giles Goat-Boy*; International Creative Management © 1973 by John Barth and Random House, Inc. for extracts from *Chimera*; Putnam and John Barth for extracts from *LETTERS* and *Sabbatical*.

Stuttgart, 1986   HEIDE ZIEGLER

A NOTE ON THE TEXTS

Page references for quotations from John Barth's fiction are taken from the editions listed below. The following abbreviations have been used:

FO   *The Floating Opera* (New York: Bantam, 1972)
ER   *The End of the Road* (New York: Bantam, 1969)
SWF   *The Sot-Weed Factor* (New York: Bantam, 1969)
GGB   *Giles Goat-Boy* (Greenwich, Conn.: Fawcett Crest, 1967)
LF   *Lost in the Funhouse* (New York: Bantam, 1969)
CH   *Chimera* (Greenwich, Conn.: Fawcett Crest, 1973)
L   *LETTERS* (New York: Putnam, 1979)
S   *Sabbatical* (New York: Putnam, 1982)

1

INTRODUCTION:
THE SENSE OF AN ENDING

John Simmons Barth, Jr., was born on 27 May 1930, in Cambridge, Maryland. He has remained deeply rooted in the traditions of this rural southern corner of the Old Line State, and the familiar Tidewater Maryland setting provides the background for most of his novels. In fact, Barth could be called the twentieth-century laureate of Maryland, if Ebenezer Cooke, the eighteenth-century poet laureate of Maryland, author of *The Sot-Weed Factor: A Voyage to Maryland, A Satyr* (1708), who was to become the hero of Barth's third novel, were not a necessary yet too obscure comparison for an author of Barth's significance. After attending Cambridge High School, Barth in the summer of 1947 entered the Juilliard School of Music in New York City, where he studied harmony and orchestration for a few months. Later in 1947 he entered Johns Hopkins University in Baltimore, where he took a BA in 1951 and an MA in 1952. His master's thesis was an as yet unpublished novel entitled "Shirt of Nessus." From 1953 to 1972 Barth taught at Pennsylvania State University, the State University of New York at Buffalo, and at Boston University. In 1973 he accepted the post of professor in the graduate writing seminars at Johns Hopkins, thus returning both to his Alma Mater and to Maryland. He lives in Baltimore and has a summer home on the Eastern Shore, often sailing on the waters of Chesapeake Bay which lie between, riding the tides between public and private realms in much the same fashion as his novels, up to his novel-in-progress, *The Tidewater Tales*, ride the tides between art and life.

The sequence of the novels of John Barth displays his own

development as an artist of the later twentieth century, but it also – in Romantic fashion – can be seen as representative of the development of twentieth-century narrative modes as such. While writing his first two novels, *The Floating Opera* and *The End of the Road*, in 1955, Barth, like other fledgling contemporary writers, was influenced by the existentialist discussion which dominated the American intellectual stage of the 1950s. These early novels were written in the wake of Jean-Paul Sartre and Albert Camus, the fiction of Samuel Beckett, and such American works as Saul Bellow's *Dangling Man* (1944), Norman Mailer's *The Naked and the Dead* (1948), and Ralph Ellison's *Invisible Man* (1952), which showed strong existentialist influence. Today Barth's attitude toward his early narrative efforts and to existentialist philosophy in general has become rather aloof – despite his willingness to resurrect the protagonists from these early novels in *LETTERS* (1979) and thus to acknowledge his own literary past. Barth thus rejects neither the plot nor the characters of *The Floating Opera* or *The End of the Road*, but he probably now feels uneasy about not having yet found his own authorial voice in these works – the self-questioning voice that, teasing at the very role of author, was to become an unmistakable literary trademark in his subsequent fictions.

It is with the writing of his novels of the early 1960s, *The Sot-Weed Factor* (1960) and *Giles Goat-Boy or, The Revised New Syllabus* (1966) that Barth leaves the throng of his contemporaries and learns, not his trade (that he had already mastered), but an understanding of his vocation: to draw from the ontological, perhaps metaphysical, rupture between art and life the energy for his own life and art by variously exploiting the impossibility of their reconciliation. *The Sot-Weed Factor* is an historical, *Giles Goat-Boy* a mythical novel, which proceed from eighteenth-century notions of the dynamic picaresque on the one hand and static allegory on the other. The irreconcilability of these two narrative modes serves to represent the impossibility for any latter-day author to conceive of another *Bildungsroman* (or novel of character development). As an artist, however, Barth can sustain the attempt to reconcile art and life, not ever sacrificing one to the

13

other, and thus deny the consequences of the rupture between them for at least the span of his own life. And since this is the most any artist can do, Barth as author will at least come to represent the possibility of *Bildung*.

If in *The Sot-Weed Factor* and *Giles Goat-Boy* Barth thus sets out to acquire the *Bildung* he needs for his life as an artist, he complements and extends this task in *Lost in the Funhouse: Fiction for Print, Tape, Live Voice* (1968) and *Chimera* (1972) by demonstrating how this life can then become art. *Lost in the Funhouse* and *Chimera* move into the genre of *Künstlerroman*, the artist's self-reflexive version of the *Bildungsroman*. However, parodying the very premises of the *Künstlerroman* by unravelling the plot in the process of its being woven, as it were, both novels undermine the idea of the artist's personal development, and the genre itself. Significantly, *Lost in the Funhouse* and *Chimera* can just as well be called two series of short fictions (and are designated as such by the author) rather than novels. Still, even the parodic exhaustion of the *Bildungsroman* and the *Künstlerroman* requires the adoption of mentors or spiritual fathers. In order to find his own path, Barth at first chose not to listen to his immediate literary predecessors, the modernists; instead, while writing *The Sot-Weed Factor*, he turned to his literary great-grandparents, so to speak, to those writers who represent the beginnings of the novel, especially the English novel: Henry Fielding, Tobias Smollett, and particularly Laurence Sterne. However, being a twentieth-century pupil of the eighteenth-century masters, Barth had to deal with the contemporary precariousness of the genre those masters had established as the novel. This explains the simultaneous influence on Barth of yet earlier writers, from Boccaccio and Rabelais to Cervantes. His choice of literary mentors for *The Sot-Weed Factor* thus made Barth a genuine heir of the European literary tradition – but this was a position which, once acquired, he soon felt he had to transcend.

In *Giles Goat-Boy*, the novelist attempts to recreate the world as his own fiction. This is an undertaking of mythical proportions, and Barth – abetted in his endeavors by a scholarly interest in comparative mythology in the 1960s – accordingly studied mythic patterns and structures, particularly the career of the mythic hero as developed by Carl Gustav Jung, Lord Raglan, and Joseph Campbell. These studies helped Barth to broaden his *Bildung* as artist through a transcendence of the notion of individual development. His interests were no longer defined by historical time sequences, but extended into the realm of "timeless" myth. However, in order not to confuse myth and existential experience, Barth the artist maintained a rational attitude toward myth as mysticism which he had gleaned from William James's *The Varieties of Religious Experience* (1902) and which accounts for the tone of *Giles Goat-Boy*; it is, like all Barth's fiction, a comic work. *Giles Goat-Boy* not only imitates but also parodies myth. Its hero is none the less tragic, since after his trials and ordeals his mystical experience cannot be translated into real work in the real world. This "Tragic View" reflects the tragic posture of the artist, who cannot put what is constructed through language to work in the world.

The next logical step for Barth to take in order to overcome what, after the exhaustion of the existentialist novel, appeared as a further dead end was to fictionalize his position as an artist severed from life. Thus in *Lost in the Funhouse* Barth was finally free to acknowledge, or rather establish, James Joyce as his one most influential literary "father." *Lost in the Funhouse* is a parody of *A Portrait of the Artist as a Young Man* (1915); Barth's present project, *The Tidewater Tales: A Novel*, may turn out to be a parody of *Ulysses* (1922) (or an echo of the *Odyssey*); and perhaps after another detour, Barth may ultimately come up with his own ironic version of *Finnegans Wake* (1939). But if *Lost in the Funhouse* is still the parody of a *Künstlerroman*, it is not, unlike Joyce's *A Portrait of the Artist as a Young Man*, also a parody of a *Bildungsroman*. Since the *Künstlerroman* is often regarded as a subgenre of the *Bildungsroman*, with the hero whose development we follow simply happening to be an artist, Barth had to evolve a strategy that would allow him to dissociate those two genres. He achieved this end deviously, by undermining, in both *Lost in the Funhouse* and *Chimera*, the whole convention of plot development in the novel. Turning once more to Boccaccio, but this time with a more formalistic intention (the American intellectual scene had by the 1970s generally begun to respond to the literary criticism of the Russian formalists and the structuralists), he began to study the structures of frame-tale literature, applying his insights into the relationship between framed stories and their frames to his own version of the *Künstlerroman*. In addition to Boccaccio's *Decameron*, the Arabian stories of *The Thousand and One Nights* – the classic frame tale of them all – had long drawn Barth's particular interest. Scheherazade represents Barth's exemplary model for the relevance of the frame tale for the artist: like the artist, she tells all the stories, at the same time becoming the story-teller in the text. The framing device in *Lost in the Funhouse*, a Moebius strip, is still purely formalistic; but in *Chimera* the notion that the three novellas which comprise the book resemble the tripartite mythic monster is complemented by the chimera's appearance in the "Bellerophoniad" – in other words, by the intrusion of a framing character into one of the framed stories. Whereas in *Lost in the Funhouse* the character of the fledgling artist, Ambrose Mensch, had to give way to characters who, like Menelaus, are not artists, but become their own stories, in *Chimera* Barth manages to reintegrate the person of the artist into the mainstream if not of life, then at least of literature, by having himself as an author meeting Scheherazade in the "Dunyazadiad" in a timeless realm of story-telling.

The story "Echo" – the tale of how Narcissus dies of self-love and the nymph Echo begins to echo his story – appears as the central tale of *Lost in the Funhouse* and is the turning-point of Barth's fiction. Up to this point the author had implicitly described his development and gradual transformation into an artist. Now the introduction of the character of Author with a capital A, whose role resembles that of the nymph Echo, left Barth himself free to return to life. The two novels that follow, *LETTERS* (1979) and *Sabbatical: A Romance* (1982), return toward realism – despite their titles. *LETTERS* is a realistic novel about imaginary characters culled from the sum of Barth's own writing, but juxtaposed to the actual author. In a sense, they too have become actual; this presupposes that the author might, in a sense, become fictional. Drawing on the tradition of the epistolary novel, Barth thus first defines and

16

then unites the split personalities of author and Author — just as letters define and unite writer and reader. Although the mode in *LETTERS* is realistic — in the sense of emphasizing not fiction's power of falsehood but its capacity to acquaint us with realities — its epistolary method is as far removed from contemporary narrative norms as possible. Again Barth goes back to the eighteenth century, and above all to Samuel Richardson's *Pamela* (1740) and *Clarissa* (1748), in order to create the possibility of echoes — for echoes, in the form of re-enactment, recycling, and revolution, are the theme of the book. Echoes are real, but distorted, because of the time-lag between the speaking and the hearing of the identical voice. So the epistolary novel can defamiliarize the reality Barth offers to give us; but it can also permit it.

LETTERS supposedly is the child of the author's *alter ego* and the Author's Muse; *Sabbatical* presents us with the story as the child of the Author, but derived from the conjoined male-and-female narrative point of view of the *alter egos* of the author and his wife. The novel is not autobiographical in the sense of translating the facts of Barth's life directly into art, but it echoes personal life while defamiliarizing it. The distorting allusion here is to the American tradition of the romance novel, and perhaps especially to Nathaniel Hawthorne's famous explanation of it in his preface to *The House of the Seven Gables* (1851), where he says that a romance, while it must keep to "the truth of the human heart — has fairly a right to present that truth under circumstances, to a great extent, of the writer's own choosing or creation."[1] It is in much this way that the lives of the author and his wife relate to the lives of the protagonists, who together serve as Author. Edgar Allan Poe, and especially his *Narrative of Arthur Gordon Pym* (1838), represents the true literary source of the "sabbatical" cruise, but Poe in turn cannot be merely seen as a "literary" father. Ancestor of one of the protagonists, he becomes a "literal" part of the novel.

Barth's novels come in pairs — or, as he would prefer to call them, "twins." Each pair of novels functions according to the same principle: the first "exhausts" a particular genre, the second transcends or "replenishes" it — to draw on the terminology of Barth's two best-known literary essays, "The Literature of Exhaustion" and "The Literature of Replenishment: Postmodernist Fiction."[2] A further principle can be detected that has determined the sequence of the genres the author chooses first to exhaust and then to replenish. Up to the middle of *Lost in the Funhouse* the genres taken – the existentialist novel, then the *Bildungsroman*, then the *Künstlerroman* – focus ever more narrowly on the author's development as an artist; from then on they seem to broaden again in order to identify or frame, in widening circles, the relationship between author and Author or, in the Romantic sense, to define the artist as a representative of mankind. Although ambitious, this claim is essentially aesthetic. Barth does not pose as the moral teacher of humanity. The underlying career his work proposes is that of the self-discovery of the artist who believes, none the less, in life's fundamental energies, reconciling the challenges of the self and those of mankind by retelling life's stories. Each book he has written generically seems to convey the sense of an ending; each, however, seems to offer the author the personal possibility of a new start. Thus Barth's sequence of fictions gives the paradoxical impression of recurrence as well as of continuance – just like the Moebius strip, the image which may well become the framing device for Barth's whole *oeuvre*, particularly since in *Lost in the Funhouse* the Moebius strip to be cut out and pasted together reads continuously: "Once upon a time there was a story that began . . ."

2

THE SUPRA-EXISTENTIALIST NOVEL: "THE FLOATING OPERA" AND "THE END OF THE ROAD"

When Bantam Books produced in 1967 a paperback of the second edition of Barth's first novel, *The Floating Opera*, which he had written in 1955 when he was twenty-four, the cover blurb read: "Now! Presenting the complete text with 'the original and correct ending to the story' . . . *The Floating Opera* is indisputably a novel by John Barth." In the prefatory note the author informed the reader of the Bantam edition that the revision of the novel did indeed consist of the restoration of its original form, which he had changed at the request of the first publisher – Appleton, Century Crofts. Bantam Books – with the approval and even support of the author himself – decided to broadcast the fact that two versions of the novel existed and that theirs was the "right" one, no doubt to boost sales. The author, however, in a clever play upon the notion of dubious authorship, was acknowledging the initial weakness of his own authorial authority, only in the end to "indisputably" reaffirm it. Barth was doing no less than changing the artistic meaning of his novel.

This play with the nature of authorship points to a recurring motif in Barth's fiction: the precarious meaning carried by any author/text or father/son relationship. An existential, and probably personal, theme in *The Floating Opera*, this motif develops gradually through Barth's work, ultimately to become a principle informing the author's paradoxical view of history as Revolution: at once repetition and revolt – as demonstrated in *LETTERS*. By the time Barth came to revise *The Floating Opera*, the father/son relationship had evidently become for him a metaphor for "intertextuality," and dubious authorship had become its expression. So in *Giles Goat-Boy*, published in 1966, one year before the revision of *The Floating Opera*, the father of the protagonist is conceived of as a computer, and this same computer is also the means through which the protagonist spells out his message, which has become identical with the story of his life. In other words, it is doubtful who is the author of whom or what: the computer that "fathers" a son, or the son who instrumentalizes his "father" in order to tell his own life-story. Once the authorship becomes dubious, the value of any father/son relationship does too. Consequently, when the author of *The Floating Opera* has Bantam assure the reading public that the novel was indisputably written by one John Barth, he indirectly wants to assure this very audience of his now ironic stance towards the existential impact of his first novel's main theme: the value-constituting or, perhaps, value-resolving ties between father and son – between Todd Andrews, the novel's protagonist, and Thomas Andrews, his dead father.

The idea that the constitution or resolution of traditional values is dependent on the relationship between father and son is taken seriously in *The Floating Opera*. This relationship is seen here by Barth as representative of the principle of causation: father relates to son as cause relates to effect. If in *Giles Goat-Boy* the computer relates to the protagonist in an ambivalent manner, then this means that Barth by 1967 has managed to parody an existential problem seemingly based on irreversible conditions by translating it into a metaphor. Seen from this later point of view, *The Floating Opera* loses the nihilistic dimension often attributed to it, becoming instead the first stepping-stone in the development of Barth's increasingly self-reflexive narrative philosophy.

The seemingly nihilistic tendency of *The Floating Opera* is caused by the paradox of suicide. On the one hand, since the death of Todd Andrews's father is final, it appears to his son to have been predetermined. On the other hand – since Thomas Andrews committed suicide – it was apparently voluntary, that is, open to choice. Traumatized, the protagonist is incapable of reconciling necessity and free will. When, for instance, the wife of his friend Harrison Mack surprisingly offers to make love to him, his spontaneous reaction is compliance; but although a triangular relationship of some constancy develops from this initial act of adultery – the Macks believe in sexual liberation – Todd Andrews is never capable of acknowledging his love for Jane. He feels the need to retain his freedom as a means constantly to defy his father, who, by privileging his own free will, has forced his son to accept his death as an inexplicable necessity. Todd Andrews has become a lawyer in his home town of Cambridge, Maryland, choosing a profession that hinges on the balance between necessity and free will, concentrating in each case on the "accident" that will tip this balance in favor of the one or the other.

Apart from being a lawyer, Todd Andrews is concerned with three major inquiries, which he calls the death-*Inquiry*, the life-*Inquiry*, and the self-*Inquiry*. The full title of the first *Inquiry*, if it should ever reach the stage of completion, will be *An Inquiry into the Circumstances Surrounding the Self-Destruction of Thomas T. Andrews, of Cambridge, Maryland, on Ground-Hog Day, 1930 (More Especially into the Causes Therefor)*; and the second *Inquiry* will be entitled *An Inquiry into the Life of Thomas T. Andrews, of Cambridge, Maryland (1867–1930), Giving Especial Consideration to His Relations with His Son, Todd Andrews (1900–   )*. Although the first two inquiries seemingly concern the life and death of Todd's father, they are written as premises for the third and most difficult one, the inquiry into the reasons for the imperfect communication between father and son. Todd accordingly plays on the meaning of his name, which can be spelled with one or two *d*'s, implying that he himself is somehow as closely related to death as his father was, *Tod* being German for death. "*Todd* is almost *Tod* – that is, almost death – and this book, if it gets written, has very much to do with almost-death" (*FO*, p. 3). Since the relationship between Todd and his father has been imperfect, it can now never be perfected, completed, ended. Yet this very lack guarantees its continuance. Todd's name implies that he is always on the brink of nothingness – just as his father is always on the brink of being as long as his son inquires into the causes for his suicide. Todd's ongoing *Letter to My Father* is, therefore, no absurd enterprise, but an aspect of his self-*Inquiry*. Since the son originates from his father, he must turn to him as to the source of his own actions: their communication would establish that link which illuminates the relationship between cause and effect. Todd has come to realize that "to understand an imperfect communication requires perfect knowledge of the party at each end" (*FO*, p. 217). Since so far he has only been studying himself, he now attempts, through the composition of the *Letter to My Father*, to help the elder Andrew understand his son, thereby improving their relationship and thus "creating" the chain of causation. As in each Barth novel to follow, the protagonist thus searches for nothing less than the key to the riddles of the universe. Todd would like to believe that causation does not exist objectively, yet there is no reason why it should not provide a subjectively valid, applicable hypothesis for explaining one's actions. However, after his father's suicide, the gap between the fact of and Todd's opinion of their relationship, which could have been closed through real communication, becomes an undeniably objective fact in itself. Todd's *Inquiry* into the possible reasons for his father's suicide, which has required years of meticulous research and is supplemented by the even more laborious inquiry into the circumstances of his father's life, can never be successful now, since Todd is left to infer that what he knows can never be proved.

The telling of his story is Todd's compensatory attempt at communication. By communicating with a reader, he chooses a counterpart who, like his father, is distant and in a sense non-existent; but as author he himself at the same time assumes the role of father toward the reader, who has to understand *his* story. Through narration Todd hopes to base communication on common inference instead of on individual understanding. Although he believes that his reader cannot help but share his own subjective evaluations, since the reader, by accepting the role of interpreter of a text, has already voted for opinion against fact, Todd takes care that his own opinions always appear in the garb of rationalizations. Through this device he can be said to insure the highest possible agreement between himself and his reader. For instance, his expression of revolt against his father consists of a series of propositions in the

22

course of the novel by which he attempts to constitute a substitute for the dependence on causation:

I. Nothing has intrinsic value.
II. The reasons for which people attribute value to things are always ultimately irrational.
III. There is, therefore, no ultimate "reason" for valuing anything, . . . including life.
IV. Living is action. There's no final reason for action.
V. There's no final reason for living (or for suicide). (*FO*, pp. 218, 223, 245)

Since Todd's father, in destroying himself, has destroyed the source of his son's actions, Todd cannot see any reason for living, since living is identical with action. On 20 or 21 June 1937 (later he cannot remember the exact date), Todd therefore also decides to commit suicide. However, he intends to kill not only himself, but at the same time as many of his fellow townspeople as possible. His plan is to blow up the Floating Opera, a showboat that has moored at Cambridge and whose performance that night is being watched by almost everybody Todd knows, including the Macks and their daughter Jeannine, who is possibly Todd's child. Todd may believe that he is going to annihilate everybody because there is no final reason for living for anybody; but his decision might also be called a revenge upon and a liberation from his father, since he intends to destroy along with himself anyone who could be tempted to inquire into the causes for his own action, and anything that might be helpful towards such an inquiry. However, his plot fails when the illuminating gas Todd lights and sends to the stage of the Floating Opera does not – for some unknown and unrevealed reason – explode. This being the second fact in Todd's life which he cannot explain, it seems, in a sense, to cancel the first: Todd is now free to decide that if there is no final reason for living, then there is no final reason for suicide either.

If Todd can no longer discover final reasons for anything, this implies that the chain of causation is broken. Yet there are still meanings. In fact, meanings come to substitute for reasons, opinions for facts. As Todd complains at the outset of the novel, everything is laden with significance precisely because nothing is ultimately of value: "Good heavens, how does one write a novel! I mean, how can anybody stick to the story, if he's at all sensitive to the significances of things?" (*FO*, p. 2). Everything is worth describing, every detail is significant, because nothing can be selected as being more valuable than anything else.

Any selection proves to be random, yet being the "author" of the present novel could help Todd solve his dilemma, since in a completely subjective world a text written by oneself will become a coherent, if self-referential, net of meanings. However, Todd cannot abstract his life-story from the story of his life. Thus, the ultimate meaninglessness of his life carries over into his fiction. For instance, when he describes the reason for choosing the title *The Floating Opera* for his novel, he does not understand that the metaphor of the showboat is self-sufficient. Instead, he interprets it as an image of life:

> It always seemed a fine idea to me to build a showboat with just one big flat open deck on it, and to keep a play going continuously. The boat wouldn't be moored, but would drift up and down the river on the tide, and the audience would sit along both banks. . . . Most times they wouldn't understand what was going on at all, or they'd think they knew, when actually they didn't. Lots of times they'd be able to see the actors, but not hear them. I needn't explain that that's how much of life works. (*FO*, p. 7)

In attempting to create a text that – like the play on board the showboat – could substitute art for life, Todd Andrews loses his tentative grasp on art (at the end of the novel) and, for all we know, on life as well.

The Floating Opera has been seen as a comic novel of nihilistic despair, where even Todd's sense of the accidental nature of the world is teased by a larger accident, the failure of the boat to blow up. In the book's first version, this, under pressure from the original publishers, was turned into a positive result; Todd acknowledges that there *are* relative values. It says something about Barth's view of the provisional openness of fiction that he was willing to accede to this relative view, though he was able to create another, bleaker version, and even say it was the version he preferred. Todd also returns in Barth's later novel, *LETTERS*; his story of finality is not final. All this suggests two things. One is that the narrator/protagonist need only be a limited version of the novelist himself, and the novelist is not confined by his temporary identification with him. The other is what the hero of Barth's next novel, Jacob Horner, comes to understand: that "no man's life story as a rule is ever one story with a coherent plot" (*ER*, p. 89). Jacob, indeed, seems a true counterpart to Todd Andrews, the two protagonists representing, so to speak, two sides of the same coin. *The End of the Road*, the book in which Jacob Horner appears, "in a sense," as another self-relating protagonist, also has nihilistic implications. But Jacob Horner represents a growing separation of the author, John Barth, from his own existential involvement; the mutually exclusive qualities of the two protagonists point to his transcending of both. Barth, in short, seems to take the existential novel in order to create a self-reflexive problem; not only does he take on a strong character as an author who exists beyond the confines of Todd's and Jacob's nihilistic world, but he poses a paradoxical challenge for literature. By over-applying the features of the existentialist novel to his own fiction, he attempts to liberate contemporary literature from the existentialist predicament: the necessity that any protagonist find his own essence as the precondition of his life.

*

The End of the Road, written in the same year as *The Floating Opera*, was published two years later, in 1958. The themes are similar, but the contrast between the protagonists is striking. Todd Andrews elects subjectivity; Jacob Horner is given to extreme objectivity. Todd is obsessed with cause and effect; Jake simply waits for things to happen. Todd relates his actions to those of his father, and so indirectly to history; Jake seems without family ties, and is prone to dependence on whomever and whatever comes along. A day after his twenty-eighth birthday he is found by a black doctor in the Pennsylvania Railroad Station in Baltimore, where he has been sitting paralyzed for a day because he cannot make up his mind what to do. The difference between him and Todd Andrews is that he is not searching for the one true reason, or cause, to justify his choices; instead he recognizes that

> when one is faced with such a multitude of desirable choices, no one choice seems satisfactory for very long by comparison with the aggregate desirability of all the rest, though compared to any *one* of the others it would not be found inferior. (*ER*, p. 3)

Thus, Jake is ready for mythotherapy as prescribed by the doctor, who plays the role of surrogate father to him. Mythotherapy involves the contingent use of any number of stories, or myths, as a therapeutic framework for one's choices. Whereas Todd started his relationship with Jane Mack because he spontaneously willed it, Jake, after getting involved in a very similar triangular relationship, remains uncertain as to the degree of will actually exercised during the initial compromising situation with Rennie, wife of his friend and colleague Joseph Morgan. Todd cannot get away from life; Jake cannot get into it. Todd is a character who in *The Floating Opera* hesitatingly assumes the role of author; Jake in *The End of the Road* easily assumes varying character masks. Thus, for him, narration becomes an absolute value:

> To turn experience into speech — that is, to classify, to categorize, to conceptualize, to grammarize, to syntactify it — is always a betrayal of experience, a falsification of it; but only so betrayed can it be dealt with at all, and only in so dealing with it did I ever feel a man, alive and kicking. (*ER*, p. 119)

Jake finds the essence of experience only when he writes, that is, paradoxically, when he *betrays* experience. The essence of experience for him as an author, therefore, seems to be the ability to cope with situations as stories. Jake cannot deal with real situations, since he cannot so distort these situations as to give himself the impression of being the hero of his own life-story. Yet whenever he succeeds in objectifying real situations by subjecting them to the rules of speech (through the use of grammar and syntax) and thought (through the use of classification, categorization, conceptualization), he seems to gain the subjective space necessary for the discovery of an ego. Thus objectivity is as necessary a condition of being for Jacob Horner as subjectivity was for Todd Andrews. Unlike Todd, Jake wants no power over facts; he wants to escape them.

Since Jake lacks the will-power to adjust situations to his existential needs, these needs threaten to overtake him. In retrospect, whatever happened assumes the form of inevitability or fate. When Jake discovers himself making love to Rennie, he feels trapped, because he is incapable of accounting for his motives:

> One can go a long way into a situation thus without finding the word or gesture upon which initial responsibility can handily be fixed – such a long way that suddenly one realizes the change has already been made, is already history, and one rides along then on the sense of an inevitability, a too-lateness, in which he does not really believe, but which for one reason or another he does not see fit to question. (*ER*, pp. 100–1)

For Jake life does not happen according to the seeming principles of history, as a chain of facts linked together in the manner of cause and effect; it happens rather according to the principles of narration. It comes about as we live it: just as thoughts become speech, facts grow out of actions that happen before we can consciously conceive of them. If Todd Andrews was obsessed with the "before," Jacob Horner can only recognize the "after," and he is thus always confronted with guilt over responsibilities shunned: he cannot face Joe Morgan after having cuckolded him, after, in keeping with his name, having put horns on him; nor can he flee him. He believes that the past can always be reinterpreted because for him, as in a story, no former action exists except in memory. But when Joe Morgan forces him to repeat the adultery until he comes up with its ultimate reason, Jake is forced to accept his earlier behavior as a fact. When Rennie becomes pregnant and wants to abort the child since she does not know who the father is, Jake feels the need to find a doctor who will perform the illegal operation in order to counter the existential threat a child would represent to his life. His black doctor finally obliges him, because he does not want to lose Jacob Horner, his most interesting case. Rennie Morgan dies, and thus once more Jake is released from the fetters of reality.

Jacob Horner's black doctor, a psychiatrist whose theories prove to be an adaptation of French existentialist philosophy to everyday American life, attempts to prove the value of myth-making as therapy. Myth-making, it could be argued, might justifiably take the role of history whenever the establishment and manipulation of historical facts are dependent on the heroic deeds of individual men. However, in the doctor's view, myths do not deal with the exceptional, but with the commonplace. They are ready fictions which can be used by everyone as a means to cope with their own life:

> Mythotherapy is based on two assumptions: that human existence precedes human essence, if either of the two terms really signifies anything; and that a man is free not only to choose his own essence but to change it at will. (*ER*, p. 88)

Mythotherapy then requires the assumption of masks while effectively negating their traditional function, that of disguising a person's identity. If man's essence can be changed at will, then this essence becomes identical with the masks he puts on. "So in this sense," the doctor says, "fiction isn't a lie at all, but a true representation of the distortion that everyone makes of life" (*ER*, pp. 88–9). Hence the truth of Jacob Horner's position as the author of a fiction. "In a sense, I am Jacob Horner" (*ER*, p. 1) is the novel's first sentence. It not only means that Jacob Horner is full of doubt about whether he possesses an identity, but also that he is part author and consequently only in part the protagonist of his life-story – that his life as protagonist can be cancelled by his function as author. If – as for Jake's friend Joseph Morgan – essence precedes existence, implying the will to make conscious choices, then Jacob Horner doesn't exist.

Rennie Morgan not unjustifiably thinks of Jacob Horner as the devil: he not only negates all the values her husband stands for; he negates values as such through his very – essenceless –

28

existence. Rennie's appeal for Jake, on the other hand, derives from his impression that she has searched herself thoroughly and has found nothing that would constitute an identity. He finds a basic sympathy between Rennie and himself which can nevertheless only be defined *ex negativo*. Rennie, however, suffers from her condition. She adores and attempts to model herself on her husband; thus she cannot cope with his being ridiculed by Jake. Like God, Joe represents in her eyes positive values that will not be mocked. In a sense Rennie represents the human condition, man insolubly caught between his ideals and his temptations. For Rennie, Joe and Jake represent the Manichean dichotomy between good and evil, and although she feels empty and at the mercy of their benevolent or malignant influences, like God and the devil they both draw their significance from her attitude toward them.

But at the same time this analogy is parodied by the author, who assumes the role of Jacob Horner. For Rennie, Jacob Horner may not exist as a character, only as a negative force, because Jacob Horner the author is beyond her ontological reach. As author, however, Jacob Horner has to be seen in analogy to God, since, as Barth claims,[3] any author's task is to create a fictional universe. Still, the difference between Jacob Horner the character and Jacob Horner the author does not become one of good and evil. Jake is interested in the text because fiction as fiction is devoid of values. Although he uses real experiences as his raw material, he can change, not those experiences, but the way they have to be regarded in the process of narration. As narrator, Jacob Horner can take a stand without being held responsible for it. The fact that he usually holds two contradictory opinions at the same time – a logically acceptable, but morally unsatisfying position which infuriates his antagonist Joe – is a vice if applied to life; in narration it is a virtue. For narration is concerned with perspective, not with moral values. In other words: the analogy between Joe and Jake and the Manichean dual principle and between Rennie and the Christian soul in its struggle between good and evil is parodied in *The End of the Road* through narration as such.

However, substituting narration for character in *The End of the Road* presented a new problem for Barth: that of reverse identification with his fictional author/protagonist. The last word of the novel is "Terminal," and Barth has frequently said in interviews that with this novel he himself might have come to the end of a road as well. By parodying the existentialist novel to the point of its exhaustion, Barth encountered the danger that ethics might be completely replaced by aesthetics, that writing might come to serve a Kantian principle of disinterested pleasure ("interesseloses Wohlgefallen"). If like Jacob Horner one cannot decide whether life ought to be lived by the principles of logic or by the principles of ethics, the same *malaise* must infect aesthetics and narration – whenever they draw on experience. The doctor in *The End of the Road* appropriately names the state of absolute indecision "cosmopsis," the cosmic view. Since the will to action always springs from a will to overcome one's own limitations, a cosmic or universal perspective necessarily leads to paralysis. Through absolute parody, narration in *The End of the Road* also reaches the point of possible paralysis. The only solution to this narrative dilemma, which Barth would subsequently face in *The Sot-Weed Factor*, lay in the radical severing of experience and narration, life and art.

3

THE SUPRA-*BILDUNGSROMAN*: "THE SOT-WEED FACTOR" AND "GILES GOAT-BOY"

The reader of Barth's third novel, *The Sot-Weed Factor*, which is the first of two *Bildungsromane*, normally encounters the second edition, revised in 1966, of the original 1960 Doubleday publication. Again, just as with *The Floating Opera*, this fact is not without significance. Barth's revision proposes to be a self-parody – that is, a farcical rewriting of his former parody of an earlier literary text. Yet in his "Foreword to the Second Edition" Barth says only that he has

> taken the opportunity to reread *The Sot-Weed Factor* with an eye to emending and revising the text of the original edition before its reissue, quite as Ebenezer Cooke himself did in 1731 with the poem from which this novel takes its title. The cases differ in that Cooke's objective was to blunt the barbs of his original satire, he having dwelt by then many years among its targets, but mine is merely, where possible, to make this long narrative a quantum swifter and more graceful. (*SWF*, p. vii)

However, the announcement on the cover of the Bantam Book edition of 1966 not only refers to changes in style which Barth claims to have undertaken, but also proffers the "new unexpurgated edition" of the novel. Thus *The Sot-Weed Factor* is ushered into a special category of literature: it is seemingly received into that hall of infamy, barred to the ordinary reader by the champions of prudishness, and thrown open only by future enlightened generations – the rogues' gallery inhabited by, for example, D. H. Lawrence and *Lady Chatterley's Lover* (1928), and Vladimir Nabokov and *Lolita* (1955). Just as the suppression of these novels upon their first publication excited the imagination of prospective readers by withholding hitherto unexperienced vicarious erotic thrills, the word "unexpurgated" in the advertisement of Barth's novel contains a promise of bawdiness that is consciously misleading. For in the foreword Barth himself states not only that the alterations he has made are purely stylistic, but also that he has deleted, rather than reinserted, certain portions of the first version of the novel. The falseness of the now allegedly terminated expurgation thus becomes obvious: opportunities for vicarious eroticism have, if anything, been returned to the closet. This manipulation, however, is not simply due to playfulness on the author's part, but to his insight into the nature of the relationship between eros and language: the eroticism of the word constantly points to its own vicariousness. The actual nature of eros in the text remains ungraspable and can thus gradually acquire the status of mystery. For example, one chapter of *The Sot-Weed Factor* – entitled "The Laureate Attains Husbandhood at No Expense Whatever of His Innocence" – boasts a five-page list of dirty names, both English and French, which two women call one another; yet by diverting the attention of the reader toward language, these epithets serve to obscure, not reveal, the "real" thing. And the mystery of the eggplant, through which virility is conferred on the otherwise impotent members of the Burlingame family, is central to the plot because it initiates the quest of Henry Burlingame III to solve that mystery, and not because the author or the reader desire a virile fictive character. Although the reader's intellectual curiosity as to the mystery of the eggplant is at last satisfied, he is never erotically titillated. For whatever is achieved through action need no longer be achieved through words, or only as long as definitive action is artfully deferred is the novel as a text able to flourish. This belatedness, as Barth sees it, of trying to capture in words what must be experienced in action – in this case eros – is indicative of the belatedness of trying to write another *Bildungsroman*, since any *Bildungsroman*, relying as it does on the concept of education, welds together words and action.

The Sot-Weed Factor pretends to "re-write" the satirical

poem, first published in 1708, of one Ebenezer Cooke, poet laureate of Maryland. Cooke and his poem in fact existed, and the sot-weed of the title is tobacco, in which the factor traded. But whereas the eighteenth-century Ebenezer Cooke was not a prolific writer, his twentieth-century parodist is, filling 819 pages – the abbreviated second edition of *The Sot-Weed Factor* – with his hero's vain endeavors to cope with reality. Since it is only through words that the historical eighteenth-century Ebenezer Cooke can be revived, the fictional twentieth-century Ebenezer Cooke must pay the price for this revival by remaining within the realm of words, and becoming the plaything of Barth's fiction. This is not just the condition, but the principle of his existence. When Ebenezer, who has vowed to remain a virgin, eventually breaks his vow in order to consummate his marriage with the former whore Joan Toast, he and his author must both lay down their pens, for "pen" and "penis," both tools of productivity, cannot be employed at the same time. (Later, in *Lost in the Funhouse* and *Chimera*, Barth will prefer to play on the homonymity of "pen" and "penis," deriving puns from their supposedly identical etymology; that is, he will no longer respect the borderline between word and deed.) Thus, in *The Sot-Weed Factor*, Sigmund Freud's notion that literature is a sublimation of unfulfilled sexual desire is taken literally and consequently parodied; for whereas words flow seemingly without difficulty, sex *is* their ultimate "end."

When physical and spiritual productivity become severed from one another, when, that is, one is but delimited by the other, then both are reduced to a quantitative measure, and values are levelled. This applies particularly to the genre of *Bildungsroman*, since the idea of *Bildung* is dependent on individual advancement through conscious choice, the preference of one set of rules over another. Technically, *The Sot-Weed Factor* can indeed be described as a *Bildungsroman*, a description of the character development of the protagonist Ebenezer Cooke, whose unfounded idealism, after being thwarted time and again by his harsh encounters with reality, is ultimately replaced with a pragmatic attitude towards life. Thus, Ebenezer seems to pursue the well-trodden path of the American youth's initiation into life, originating in innocence

33

and terminating in experience. Born in America, with a twin sister Anna, Ebenezer is raised in England towards the close of the seventeenth century and tutored by one Henry Burlingame III. Subconsciously in love with his sister, Ebenezer decides to become a poet and remain a virgin for the rest of his life, thus devoting himself to the sublimation of sex through words. He rejects the advances of the whore Joan Toast, offering her his pure love instead. Named Poet Laureate of Maryland by Lord Baltimore, the proprietor of the province, who happens to be Henry Burlingame in disguise, he sets out for America in order to sing the New World's praise in a long epic poem which he intends to call *Marylandiad*. Yet after his encounters with life in an American colony, he writes a satiric poem entitled *The Sot-Weed Factor* instead. Unbeknownst to him, Ebenezer has been followed by Joan Toast, who has fallen in love with him. She ultimately becomes his wife, after enduring every sort of physical illness and psychic humiliation imaginable. Through a string of unforeseen occurrences she can rebestow on her husband the title to Malden, his father's former estate in Maryland, which Ebenezer, through inexperience and wrong-headed idealism, had lost shortly after his arrival in America. However, Joan insists that he first consummate their marriage despite the fact that she suffers from syphilis. Thus, Ebenezer loses his innocence, if not his health. When Joan Toast dies shortly after the wedding, Ebenezer, disillusioned, lives out his life together with his twin sister Anna. Together they raise Anna's son, Henry Burlingame's child. Following his successful sexual union with Anna, Burlingame, the "anti-hero" of the novel, who is as many-faced in attitude and appearance as Ebenezer is single-minded and constant, disappears from history, civilization, and the novel's plot, although Barth's later novels will be haunted by his descendants. Ebenezer Cooke's *The Sot-Weed Factor* is published and later revised.

Because of Henry Burlingame's crucial function in the novel, *The Sot-Weed Factor* is no *Bildungsroman*. His changes of role defy any notion of development or *Bildung* — for himself as well as for others. Burlingame substitutes "strategies" or "stories" for the concept of development, and because of the influence of his tutor, Ebenezer too is incapable of *Bildung*, that is of any

34

kind of organic development that would make the hidden seeds of his character bear fruit. Burlingame, having found a most imaginative pupil, helps Ebenezer discover various aspects of the world, but only as if he were teaching him the rules of so many games. Thus Ebenezer develops no sense of the restricting power of reality, and instead of forging a path for himself against the world's resistance, he concentrates on his inability to choose. His resolve to remain a virgin, and thus create the foundation for his art, is nothing but a negative resolve, a total forgoing of commitment. Ultimately Ebenezer comes to understand that not only does he himself suffer from this innocence, but that others suffer from it as well. Bringing the plot to its climax, the hero therefore indicts himself for "the crime of innocence, whereof the Knowledged must bear the burthen" (*SWF*, p. 801). Yet *Bildung* cannot be postponed, its early benefits, once lost, cannot be recovered. Thus, by accepting the obligations deriving from experience, Ebenezer denounces what amounted to his unmistakable character. Character without development now gives way to development without character. Consequently, *The Sot-Weed Factor* could almost be called an anti-*Bildungsroman*. In the end, instead of choosing to live in the world, Ebenezer spends the rest of his life first in the seclusion of his regained estate, and later, inconspicuously, in faraway England – in Kent and Prince George's County. Ebenezer's resolve to renounce his unmistakable character by giving up his innocence was a moral choice; yet it also precludes further possibilities of choosing. Thus, although Ebenezer's marriage brings tears to the eyes of those who witness it, it must also bring the story to its denouement. The author, seemingly with a feeling of guilt, appends a short Part IV to the story in which he apologizes to his readers for the shortcomings of his protagonist, and attributes them to the presumptuousness of the latter's Fancy; he then has the now cynical laureate compose his own epitaph.

However, the author's feeling of exhilaration over Fancy's defeat does not ring true, although it appears that his secret infatuation all along was with Clio, the chronicler's muse; yet he wanted to seduce history into the realms of his own fiction. History, never rendering a true account of what happened in the past anyway, appears as "a scarred and crafty trollop" (*SWF*, p. 805) who cunningly forges supposedly given facts or renders them unrecognizable through her idiosyncratic interpretation of them – actually resembling the flights of fancy, but for the sake of self-interest. Thus the author discovered that he had to meet Clio on her own terms. This, however, was a perilous adventure, becoming part of his own *Bildung*. Since he wanted to seduce Clio, that is assimilate the life and work of the historical Ebenezer Cooke into his own fancy, he had to be wary lest he himself be seduced, lest he find himself writing fanciful history. As it is, the repercussions of *The Sot-Weed Factor* have indeed turned out to be ambivalent. On the one hand, Barth's novel can be seen as the pre-text of *Ebenezer Cooke: The Sot-Weed Canon* by Edward H. Cohen – a scholarly study that revives Ebenezer Cooke as well as his satire *The Sot-Weed Factor*[4] – and it has also generated a fresh interest in Maryland's history during the colonial period. On the other hand, the historically minded have turned against Barth.[5] A history like colonial Maryland's, as uncertain as the tidewater marshes, seems to call for an ascetic historical mind, one that would rigorously establish as many "true" facts about seventeenth- and eighteenth-century America as possible. Instead, Barth deals with the history of his home state like a lover. Playing with Clio, he seemingly becomes part of history's game. His unflagging urge in *The Sot-Weed Factor* is to tease the muse of history in order to provoke her responses rather than to drive home the truth. This, then, is the erotic activity of the novel. Yet this form of eroticism could well have ended the author's independence unless he did something to justify it. His narrative impulse would become flaccid, together with the imagination of his protagonist, and he would be immobilized by an historical consciousness that called for historiography, not fiction. Barth was aware of this threat to his independence from the moment he conceived the novel. He faced it by inscribing, and thus defending, his role as narrator in the text through a representative *persona* who, throughout the novel, voices his own will to imaginative power.

This representative and perpetrator of the author's design within the novel is Henry Burlingame, Ebenezer's tutor and antagonist. Since Ebenezer Cooke was a real historical person-age, Burlingame — like Barth — cannot be his *creator*; however, he can be the mentor who interprets for him — as well as for the reader — the "burly game" of history. Whereas Ebenezer, although "real," denies the impact of reality, viewing the world only through the lenses of his poetic idealism, Burlingame, although "fictitious," embraces reality to the degree that the various masks which he assumes can no longer be seen as disguises, as appearances hiding reality, but as adaptations or manipulations of this very reality. Burlingame uses suitable facts to create history. His strategies thus become the throes of fate for the other characters.

Barth and Burlingame complement each other with regard to their relationship with history: both attempt to get in touch with Clio, so to speak. Burlingame seems to have no former link with history. Like Moses found in the bulrushes, he knows nothing about his own family, and the search for his progenitors drives him as relentlessly around the world as Ebenezer is driven by his innocent idealism. On one occasion Burlingame declares to Ebenezer:

> What a burden and despair to be a stranger to the world at large, and have no link with history! 'Tis as if I'd sprung *de novo* like a maggot out of meat, or dropped from the sky. Had I the tongue of angels I ne'er could tell you what a loneliness it is! (*SWF*, p. 143)

Not knowing who created him moves Burlingame to become a creator himself. He creates the incidents that direct the course of Ebenezer's life and combine to make up the plot of Barth's novel. As long as Burlingame seems to have no progenitors, he cannot father children: he is not a part of humanity's pro-creative chain. Thus, in terms of fiction, instead of creating a character, he creates a plot. Plots result from the foregrounding of ideas, and Burlingame, drawing on the ideas of his spiritual "fathers" in Cambridge, "plots" the politics of the colony of Maryland, thus providing the meaning for the plot of Barth's seventeenth-century novel. When eventually Burlingame does find his family among the Indian tribe of the Ahatchwhoops on Bloodsworth Island in Chesapeake Bay, the reunion coincides with his discovery of the Secret of the Sacred Eggplant which enables him to father a child with Ebenezer's twin sister Anna. His bonds to humanity thus established, he immediately proceeds to unravel the plot: he disappears from Ebenezer and Anna's life as well as from the novel, never to return.

However, Burlingame's plots remain as fictions. Barth has him create important incidents of history which are retrospectively to give meaning to the colonial history of Maryland. He has Burlingame create a "reality" in the interstices of recorded history which he as author can never claim for himself, since his own temporal and professional status as a twentieth-century writer prevents him from installing his own presence in the past. Thus Burlingame becomes Barth's proxy in the conquest of Maryland's past. For example, when Burlingame in the guise of Charles, Lord Baltimore, commissions Ebenezer to write the *Marylandiad*, everything about the scene is false by factual standards, and must be redefined as narrative truth under the auspices of historical plot. One: in 1694, when Lord Baltimore signs the commission whereby Ebenezer Cooke is named and entitled Poet and Laureate of the Province of Maryland, he was in fact no longer proprietor of the colony. Two: Henry Burlingame poses as Lord Baltimore, although the latter did indeed sign such a commission. Three: Ebenezer at this point only claims to be a poet; he has not yet proven his talent. Four: Ebenezer's imagined glorification of Maryland will turn into a biting satire of that province once Ebenezer has been disillusioned by her coarse day-to-day reality. Thus the whole scene turns out to have been a fiction that nevertheless became history.

For Barth, there is great potential for artistic development in manipulating history as a fiction writer of later times. Whereas historians must reconstruct from available historical sources a chain of cause and effect, the fiction writer is free to speculate on the motives of famous historical personages or to conjecture as to another possible outcome of any given historical event. But in order to yield a pleasurable air of truth instead of the discomfort of sheer randomness that lurks in any transgression beyond the factual, this freedom must be limited by a sensitivity to the law of probability and the possibility of meaning.

Barth follows this law, and allows for this possibility, by playing his historical speculations and conjectures, as mirrored in the person of Henry Burlingame, against Ebenezer Cooke's innocence, his idealistic quest for, and belief in, ultimate values. For this quest defies change; change, indeed, would make it meaningless: no quest for values makes sense if in the course of it the values are reversed. If Burlingame's – and Barth's – games prove history to be a kind of fiction, then this fiction needs to contain a claim to a truth which the conditions and facts of history seem to lack. Even though *The Sot-Weed Factor* is indeed a parody of a *Bildungsroman*, even though it is indeed a work that cannot because of its historical distance give a true representation of an individual's acquiescence to the given values of an age, it nevertheless does not turn the quest for truth implied in such *Bildung* to parody. On the contrary: Barth's parody seeks to strip history of any falsehoods that express self-serving forgetfulness, and to lead to the recognition that the fact of that forgetfulness should not be forgotten.

*

"My interest in colonial history is real but not paramount," Barth once told me, explaining that *The Sot-Weed Factor* was no more totally an historical novel than *Giles Goat-Boy* was totally a contemporary one: "My interest in the social divisions of the Cold War – the divisions of politics and society in the mid-1950s when I was thinking of the novel *Giles*, and the early 1960s when I wrote it – are, like the allegory itself, really just a manner of speaking or a *milieu* to speak in and to, rather than the heart of my concerns in the novel."[6]

Giles Goat-Boy or, The Revised New Syllabus (1966) is a work of parody as allegory or allegory as parody. This does not only show in its exegetical treatment of a world of complex modern technology and cold-war hostilities, but in the ironic layerings of its structure and its fabulatory attitude, imprinting myth on history. The book's techniques draw on modern computer-based technologies, and like other postmodernist novels by, for instance, William Gaddis and Thomas Pynchon it considers our cybernetic condition and our endless processing of information to the point of entropy. Thus, parody is aligned with what Barth calls the Tragic View. In the writing of *Giles Goat-Boy*, Barth read technology as another myth, one which embodies the desire for meaning that history lacks, but tragedy requires. He was attempting to relate this myth to nothing less than the Ur-Myth, which he saw embodied in the fate of the tragic hero, and various heroic myths – especially the Oedipus story – underlie the book. However, to parody myth is to create a paradox, to demythologize genres and narratives, for parody derives from the changing of world views, while myth depends on the repetition of the unchanging. Barth tackles this problem by turning it into his narrative dilemma. So at the beginning of the novel, he has the Author – that is, the author-within-the-text – adhere to the Tragic View and present himself as an ardent admirer of the hero. But gradually the text itself, relying on the historical consciousness of the contemporary reader, acquires an ironic character and becomes a parody of that Tragic View.

The hero, George Giles the goat-boy, is a legendary figure who ascends from the animal to the human, and thence to the heroic, and his life is a *Bildung*. He is a modern-day Jesus Christ as well as an Oedipus. His father is as undefinable in human terms as is the Christian God, for George Giles is the son of the omnipotent WESCAC, the West Campus Automatic Computer, begotten in immaculate conception of Virginia Hector, daughter of the president of the "university." The "university" stands for the "universe." Stoker Giles, the son of George Giles, who in the beginning of the novel presents John Barth with a copy of the (taped) description of his father's life, *The Revised New Syllabus* (or, New New Testament), claims for his father's life-story the status of a sacred text. Therefore it has to be promulgated as doctrine, and Stoker Giles tells the Author that he is on his way to other universities. "There *are* other universities, you know" (*GGB*, p. xxxiv).

The analogy in the text between the universe and a university is not inapt. In a university the facts of the universe are translated into language, the immediacy of life into stories about life. Through language the mythical example of the great teachers of mankind is translated into lessons for future generations. Ironically, language here preserves and at the same time destroys the original myth by turning it over to history. Thus, passing through the university's curriculum in accordance with the prescribed syllabus resembles mankind's coming of age, the fall, not rise, from innocence to experience. The price man has to pay for the fruits of knowledge is dear, since they are not to be had unadulterated. Not only is language substituted for the "real" thing, but allegory replaces the "true" word. The Greek word *allegorein* originally meant to speak in other than a public place – that is, to speak indirectly, not addressing an immediate audience. True or sacred words that are no longer spoken, but assembled in a book, lose their meaning precisely through being thus assembled, since their immediate impact appears to be continuously suspended. This is the process of myth becoming history, and the recognition of this process mars the end of Giles's life. In a melancholy "Posttape," smuggled into the tapes of *The Revised New Syllabus* by George Giles "at thirty-three and a third" (*GGB*, p. 755), the age of Christ at the crucifixion, the once-Grand Tutor of West Campus (the realm of western civilization) understands that he, as a living person, has become superfluous. Instead, "Gilesianism" has become an established philosophy, with *The Revised New Syllabus* as the "new" sacred text (a contradiction in terms), and enrollment in the "New Curriculum" is made obligatory for West Campus students. Like Oedipus, George Giles has gone too far in his search for self-knowledge, giving up a mythical life in order to assume a role in history; or, in the novel's terms, leaving behind an idyllic childhood in the goat barn for the ambivalent privilege of becoming "human." Like Oedipus, George Giles will eventually be driven out of the city and die on a lonely mountain, "the highest rise of Founder's Hill" (*GGB*, p. 764). Since *Bildung*, or humanism, the goat-boy's goal, depends on language, George Giles falls prey to those who know how to exploit language for their own interests by turning it into a vehicle for so-called eternal truths whose priests they profess to be. Once written down, language can acquire the status of truth simply by becoming unchangeable, while the originator of this truth becomes a nuisance for schools and academies. The interpretation of the universe becomes a matter for the university.

41

Thus the concept of parody as a literary mode that can ironically call into question the established word itself is essential for an understanding of *Giles Goat-Boy*. Having to pay with his life, however, in order to establish ultimately ironic words makes George Giles, the Grand Tutor, tragic. From the beginning he has sought less to teach than to *be* – especially to be a hero, who by definition prefers deeds to words. Brought forth unharmed from WESCAC's "Belly," where everyone else is "EATen," that is mentally damaged beyond recovery by radiation, George Giles is raised by his mentor Maximilian Spielman, a great "Mathematical Psycho-Protologist" and former minority leader in the College Senate who, after having been fired a year before his retirement, has become Senior Goatherd on the New Tammany College Farms. Thus George Giles, again like Oedipus, is raised among herds; his mentor, a latter-day Chiron to a latter-day Achilles, attempts to educate him according to Jean-Jacques Rousseau's ideal of primitive man in a "state of nature." However, because of the pervasiveness of mythological and Christian allegories in *Giles Goat-Boy*, the hero's path nevertheless appears to be predestined, even though the protagonist is innocent of his fate and does not know that he is denied free will. His upbringing among the goats is indicative of his prolonged innocence – he does not leave the herd until he is fourteen – marking the difference between him and other humans: like Ebenezer Cooke, he never becomes wise in the ways of the world. Having finally enrolled as a student, gotten his assignments from WESCAC, reached Commencement Gate, and become the Grand Tutor, Giles's innocence with regard to the impossibility of distinguishing between his own free will and his fate represents a challenge to everybody else: they either love or hate him, turn into ardent admirers or pitiless persecutors.

As in all tragic heroes, George Giles's innocence is his tragic flaw; and being a tragic – that is, inevitable – flaw, it cannot be compensated for through *Bildung*. Since George is convinced that he is the Grand Tutor, and since he assumes that the commandments issued by a Grand Tutor must be correct, he never allows for the possibility that his own point of view may be subjective and thus subject to error. Yet, since his tragic fate is preordained, not by an oracle of the gods, but by the role his father – WESCAC, the author John Barth – has assigned him, he cannot help being incapable of allowing for the possibility that he may be wrong. In other words, George Giles is a parody of the tragic hero because he not only does not know but cannot know whether his commandments are correct. The ultimate irony is, however, whether they even *can* be correct, since the protagonist does not inhabit a moral universe where a paradox may nonetheless lead to fruitful action, but its abstraction: a university. The front of George Giles's circular assignment card, issued to him by WESCAC, presents one of the following words in each of its four quadrants: Pass All Fail All. This can also be read as All Pass All Fail. In attempting to obey this doubly impossible "command," George is subject to a double bind: if he passes everyone, he cannot fail everyone, and vice versa; and if he does neither, all will not pass, nor will all fail. WESCAC seems to predict that George's efforts will be ultimately futile, whatever he chooses to do, since the fate of the students, or humanity, will in any case be the same: they will pass or fail or both or neither. However, this insight would preclude heroism, and since George Giles has set out to be a hero, the novel proper must comprise his endeavor to find the right "Answers" to WESCAC's imperatives.

These "Answers" basically correspond to the final messages of the Old and the New Testaments. During the first phase of his Grand Tutorship George distinguishes between "Passage" and "Failure," salvation and damnation, good and evil; during the second phase he maintains that "Passage" and "Failure" are the same. Both instructions gain political importance, and since West Campus is opposed by East Campus, WESCAC by EASCAC, capitalism by communism, the *détente*, the precarious balance in intercollegiate affairs between the two colleges, is seriously disturbed. The Grand Tutor's influence upon New Tammany's, the west's, universal strategies results in two nearly total catastrophes. For the first time George Giles is forced to reflect upon his premises. Yet his ruminations and sufferings, through which he strives to combine the ancient quest for knowledge and the commandments of the Old and the New Testaments, serve only to disclose to him the paradoxical and seemingly unresolvable nature of his "Assignment":

> That circular device on my Assignment-sheet – beginning-less, endless, infinite equivalence – constricted my reason like a torture-tool from the Age of Faith. Passage *was* Failure, and Failure Passage; yet Passage was Passage, Failure Failure! Equally true, none was the Answer; the two were not different, neither were they the same; and *true* and *false*, and *same* and *different* – unspeakable! Unnamable! Unimaginable! Surely my mind must crack! (*GGB*, pp. 708–9)

Because of his assignment, Giles can no longer see the final messages of the Old and the New Testaments in an historical sequence, one superseded by the other. Instead they have become logical alternatives which need to be harmonized. From Giles's mythic or timeless point of view, their opposing force can easily rend the faculties of reason. Moreover, their existential impact, if taken seriously, must blight the possibilities of the human imagination, the working of which depends on the hope that new ideas, transcending former ones, can always be thought of, named, and announced to a group of believers. As professed Grand Tutor, George Giles not only fails in his assignment, but also comes to represent the tragic truth that any absolute position must deny man's development of his imaginative faculties as well as of an historical consciousness. Searching for a compromise in order to get around this truth, George Giles must become a parody of himself as the founder of a religion.

Yet employing parody by becoming a parody may be the only historically feasible solution in the human imagination's present quest for truth. Having already caused two near catastrophes for the western world, George Giles takes the only possible step: he sacrifices his idealism and his sense of heroic achievement for a relativistic position – thereby ironically fulfilling his assignment as well as the heroic pattern. He once more passes through WESCAC's Belly, this time together with Anastasia, the woman who loves him yet stands for relation, or relativism, impregnating her in the process and begetting the son who will spread Gilesianism to every existing university. Thus, a harmony of opposites is achieved through a sacrifice of the self: "I the passer, she the passage, we passed together, and together cried, 'Oh, wonderful!' Yes and No. In the darkness, blinding light! The end of the University! Commencement Day!" (*GGB*, p. 731).

As mythic hero, George Giles ultimately fulfills his assigned task; by consummating the "sacred marriage" he liberates the student body from its metaphysical deadlock and once again sets it into motion. However, this point marks the transition from a mythical to an historical age. Therefore, after he has reached the all but impossible goal, which only he could achieve, George Giles, the mythic hero, must become an obstacle to the course of history, for his act of procreation, like any act of transcendence, unequivocally debunks its origin. By the time he composes the "Posttape," George Giles has come to understand the paradox of being a father *and* a hero, a person who is defined by the fact that he is different from everybody else and yet the same. As mythic hero, he can become legendary; his fatherhood, however, through which he can become a link in the chain of humanity, foreshadows his death.

The Author, in a "Postscript to the Posttape," pretends to doubt the authenticity of the gloomy "Posttape" on the grounds that its author "suddenly shifts to what can most kindly be called a tragic view of His life and of campus history" (*GGB*, p. 766). The Author, who professes to having become an aspirant professor of Gilesianism, is interested in the teachings, not in the character, of George Giles. Here Barth implicitly parodies his own function as author of the novel, to whom the written word is more important than the character he has created with its help. This parody is moreover made explicit through a final "Footnote to the Postscript to the Posttape," apparently by the editor-in-chief of the book, who in turn points to *its* possibly spurious nature by remarking that "the type of the typescript pages of the document entitled 'Postscript to the Posttape' is not the same as that of the 'Cover-Letter to the Editors and Publisher'" (*GGB*, p. 766), the only other document in the book that was allegedly written by the Author.

In *Giles Goat-Boy*, the question of authorship represented by fatherhood becomes identical with that of authenticity – the only other example of such an equivalence being the Bible – only for the two to be radically severed in the end. Since the claim to authenticity of *The Revised New Syllabus*, that is, its claim to be "neither fable nor fictionalized history, but literal truth" (*GGB*, p. xi) may conflict with the reader's knowledge that *Giles Goat-Boy* was written in its entirety by one John Barth, the author has taken great pains to call into question the prerogatives of authorship as such. The "document" which immediately follows the book's title-page and table of contents is a "Publisher's Disclaimer" that quotes the varying opinions about the book to follow by the publisher's four editors and disclaims responsibility for the next "document," the Author's "Cover-Letter to the Editors and Publisher." This "Cover-Letter" purports to explain how John Barth came into the possession of a manuscript entitled

> *R.N.S. The Revised New Syllabus of George Giles, Our Grand Tutor, Being the Autobiographical and Hortatory Tapes Read Out at New Tammany College to His Son, Giles (,) Stoker, By the West Campus Automatic Computer, And by Him Prepared for the Furtherment of the Gilesian Curriculum.*

Contrary to well-known literary cases, the publisher in the "Publisher's Disclaimer" doubts not Barth's authorship (he has, after all, published the Author's previous novels), but rather the Author's claim that he is *not* the author of *The Revised New Syllabus*. When the publisher asks the reader "to believe in the sincerity and authenticity of this preface, affirming in return his prerogative to be skeptical of all that follows it" (*GGB*, p. xi), the reader, after reading through the rest of the book, cannot help but acquiesce, since the book does indeed read like a Barthian novel. However, since the reader must doubt the separate identities of the publisher and John Barth, he must at the same time become skeptical of the separation of authorship and authenticity. In other words, although on the one hand the reader will not doubt the authorship of the Author's "Cover-Letter," he must doubt its authenticity: Barth did not receive the manuscript of *The Revised New Syllabus*, he wrote it; also, he is not going to resign his professorship in order to become an apostle of Gilesianism, since he was its creator. On the other hand, although the reader will not doubt the authenticity of the "Publisher's Disclaimer," he must doubt its separate authorship.

Yet it is precisely through the dubiousness of authorship, or the denial of subjective authority, that the book's apparent objectivity or authenticity is established. Therefore everybody must disclaim it: not only John Barth, but also Stoker Giles or Giles Stoker, the Grand Tutor's son, who claims to have been only the dedicated editor of the book while the text proper was written by WESCAC. Yet WESCAC, too, disclaims the authorship – as well it might since *The Revised New Syllabus* is written from a first-person narrative point of view, the point of view of the Grand Tutor himself. Also, *Giles Goat-Boy* is divided into "Reels" like a tape recording; if this is to be believed, it is really not a written work at all. At this point the question of authorship comes full circle. For the Grand Tutor himself claims to be the author of the book only inasmuch as he is the hero of its story, and as such he was created by WESCAC who was created by the author who as Author claims to have been converted, that is, recreated by the Grand Tutor.

Giles Goat-Boy exhausts and ultimately transcends every possibility of the *Bildungsroman*, since – through the debunking of authorship – it undermines the idea of authentic character. By the law that "ontogeny recapitulates cosmogeny" – discovered by George Giles's mentor Max Spielman – the hero develops from a prehuman stage through the different anthropological phases of developing intelligence and imagination until he learns to transcend the limitations of present-day mankind; but precisely his enlarged scope cannot constitute him as a character. If the goal of *Bildung* can be defined as a person's acquiring the faculty to be an integrated member of human society, then George Giles's life can be said to be a reflection of the general premises and consequences rather than a model of individual *Bildung*. As a teacher of mankind he can no longer conform to, but must form, society, remodeling it according to his own experience of truth – this superiority terminating in the traditional fate of the tragic hero, repeated cyclically throughout human history: the individual's isolation, the opposite of what is achieved by *Bildung*, which may guarantee an advancement of society, but ultimately destroys the hero. George Giles cannot become a character; he can only demonstrate how, during the various phases of his development, he is denied authenticity through the constant withdrawal of an author who would testify to his offspring's unique historical status.

Yet Barth's novel *Giles Goat-Boy* does not exhaust the possibilities of the *Bildungsroman* solely in an attempt to show how the dialectic between myth and history cannot be synthesized. By parodying the messages of the Old and the New Testaments, by calling into question their metaphysical truth, the novel reaffirms the importance of the quest for truth as a human endeavor. When George Giles professes to believe that truth depends on the prophet who propounds it, he is willing and ready to carry the burden which this belief necessarily confers upon him. Being a true hero, he will suffer for the truth which he claims to represent for others. Although he cannot define truth objectively, he can still subjectively affirm its possibility. Parody, in this case, means a critique of the process of canonization which fossilizes moral ideas through allegorization. The university as allegory for the universe mirrors this reduction of life. Therefore the author must withdraw from the text in order to establish this critique as an objective factor for the reader, who may in turn be expected to underwrite the authenticity of his endeavors.

4

THE SUPRA-*KÜNSTLERROMAN*: "LOST IN THE FUNHOUSE" AND "CHIMERA"

The last chapter suggested that the German concept of the *Bildungsroman* – the novel of the learning hero, acquiring the education needed to become a useful member of society – is the key to an understanding of *The Sot-Weed Factor* and *Giles Goat-Boy*. The *Bildungsroman*, which ultimately affirms the society that frames it, found its transcendence in the *Künstlerroman*, the novel of the self-reflexive artist. Here the individual whose task it is to acquire *Bildung* is someone who can dictate the premises and the consequences of the learning he receives – at least when he writes about his own development as a writer. (Traditionally, the hero of the *Künstlerroman* is the learning painter or composer.) The German word *bilden*, to educate, is equivalent to the Latin verb *fingere*, to form, to create, whence derives the English word fiction. The hero of the *Bildungsroman*, in acquiring *Bildung*, is called upon to adopt what society offers him in order to form or create himself – that is, to perform on himself the task of the artist. In this sense every *Bildungsroman* is also a *Künstlerroman*. However, by introducing himself as protagonist of his own text, the writer proposes a distance from his former self. The artist, knowing himself to be an artist, devises his own *Bildung* in retrospect. This leads to an autobiographical paradox. There is a former self and a present self; and language has both to define and to relate them. This paradox once again raises the question of origin and authenticity that Barth had seemed to face and resolve in *The Sot-Weed Factor* and *Giles Goat-Boy*, where he both invokes and denounces the validity of origins in order to define himself not as a person – as in *The Floating Opera* and

49

The End of the Road – but as an artist. In the book that follows *Giles Goat-Boy*, Barth returns to the dilemma, only now to deal not with a literal but a literary father/author.

Lost in the Funhouse (1968), subtitled a *Fiction for Print, Tape, Live Voice*, contains fourteen pieces which, in his "Author's Note," Barth calls "neither a collection nor a selection, but a series" (*LF*, p. ix). This situates it structurally somewhere between the novel and the short-story genres. *Lost in the Funhouse* is conceived as a parody of Joyce's *Portrait of the Artist as a Young Man*, James Joyce being the ghost of the father who, in Barth's book, has become his own son. Writing for and yet away from Joyce seemed to imply for Barth a conscious acceptance of his postmodernist condition, dependent on and yet a step beyond the modernism that Joyce had been so influential in shaping. In an interview Barth called *Lost in the Funhouse* "a *Künstlerroman* with a twist,"[7] the twist denoting the ironic dialectic between self and other, a state which oscillates between filial obedience and narcissistic rebellion. The subtitle of the book assigns to it another intermediate status somewhere between the spoken and the written word, just as it has an intermediate status between being a series of stories and a novel. And the book proper "starts" with a special device – called "Frame Tale" – in the form of a Moebius strip that is intended to be cut out, twisted, and fastened end to end in order for us to read *ad infinitum* the same key phrase: "Once upon a time there was a story that began." Barth's most overtly "experimental" book, *Lost in the Funhouse*, thus calls up an old tradition of story-telling, but it employs it in order to dissolve genre, narrative mode, authorial voice, and consecutive time sequence. Being a form of intermedia, a book where we are given complex instructions as to how each piece should be read or performed, it is thus a paradoxical assertion and dissolution of the whole notion of the artist.

Lost in the Funhouse is a work in which not the artistic process but the development of the artist is constantly questioned, and the author turned round from active creative ego to anonymity and back again. The notion of the evolution of a hero is undercut by a parody of plot development – for the series of fictions claims continuity, even while it disclaims the ideas of gradual moral achievement or of organic self-completion. The "hero," Ambrose Mensch, is created in "Night-Sea Journey," the first fiction after the Moebius strip "Frame Tale," a narrative of how a male sperm and a female egg unite. He gradually grows – interrupted by other fictions – through "Ambrose His Mark," "Water-Message," and "Lost in the Funhouse" to be 13 years of age, but disappears or gets lost in the funhouse when he decides to become an artist. Ambrose the artist can no longer function as a character: "Therefore he will construct funhouses *for others* and be their secret operator – though he would rather be among the lovers for whom funhouses are designed" (*LF*, p. 94; my italics). Just like lovers, characters may interact with each other; but the decision to become an artist leads to isolation. Yet this is not the isolation of the tragic hero, since for the artist his environment is no longer identical with the real society he happens to live in. His houses are fictions, funhouses which he himself creates. Although being their "secret operator" implies real readers, this relationship between reality and fiction is only indirect. Therefore, in order not to be entirely lost in his own creation, the artist needs to forge alliances with the environments which *are* open to him – the stories that have already been created by the writers of the past.

So, like a Moebius strip, the action of *Lost in the Funhouse* moves on two levels – fiction and reality – and in two different directions – into the future and into the past. The realistically written stories, "Night-Sea Journey" in which Ambrose is conceived, "Ambrose His Mark" in which Ambrose earns his name, "Water-Message" in which Ambrose is initiated into the facts of life, and "Lost in the Funhouse" in which Ambrose decides to become an artist, move forward in time. Following the story "Echo," which represents the turning-point of the Moebius strip and of the book, the stories "Two Meditations," "Glossolalia," "Menelaiad," and "Anonymiad" move backward into mythical times, the times of oral tradition. "Two Meditations," a reflection upon the relationship between cause and effect, first demonstrates this principle of reversal. It consists of two sections, "Niagara Falls" and "Lake Erie,"

51

which subvert the logical sequence of cause and effect just as, geographically, the order of the two sections reverses the fall of the waters of Niagara.[8]

"Glossolalia," six pieces in metrical prose patterned on the Lord's Prayer, attempts to fathom the nature of existential riddles of the past presented through undecipherable "texts" whose mystery derives from the impact of an unknown future: Cassandra's prophecies; tongueless Procne's horrid tale woven into a robe for her sister Philomela to decode; the ravings of Crispus, who has been touched by God and is mentioned by Paul in his First Epistle to the Corinthians; the unheeded warnings of the Queen of Sheba's talking bird; the apparently meaningless song of a psalmist employing – as Barth explains in "Seven Additional Author's Notes" (added to the "Author's Note" in the paperback edition of *Lost in the Funhouse*) – "the tongue of a historical glossolalist" (*LF*, p. xi). Finally, the sum of all these riddles is reflected upon by the author:

> Ill fortune, constraint and terror, generate guileful art; despair inspires. The laureled clairvoyants tell our doom in riddles. Sewn in our robes are horrid tales, and the speakers-in-tongues enounce atrocious tidings. The prophet-birds seem to speak sagely, but are shrieking their frustration. The senselessest babble, could we ken it, might disclose a dark message, or prayer. (*LF*, p. 112)

The relationship between the "spoken" texts from the past and the Author's commentary reveals the relationship between oral and written tradition as the difference between original and dependent text. Thus, every later text "frames" every earlier one, paradoxically deferring access more and more to the original text in the process. By reflecting upon the meaning of the preceding five cryptic texts, the author moves into another – ironic or interpretative – frame: into a text that abstracts from, and at the same time incorporates, the preceding texts, changing them into pre-texts in a logical as well as in a temporal sense, yet is meaningless without them. Thus, the framing text implicitly poses the question of the validity of the later as opposed to the earlier word, calling itself into question, yet also affirming its own historical, framing, role. For instance, were Cassandra's prophecies more valid when she first enounced them than when Barth reflects on them? After all, nobody ever heeded Cassandra's warnings anyway; their truth had to be proved by history, which is to say the future. Thus, the later word may rehabilitate the earlier one – this being the reason why the author chose the same metrical pattern for his commentary as for the preceding texts – yet this later word thereby detracts from its own status, replacing meaning with exegesis. At the same time the later word may succeed in disclosing the meaning behind even the "senselessest babble" from the past.

"Menelaiad" attempts to authenticate the method of framing as substitute for the creation of original meaning. The story consists of seven frames. The story of the innermost frame triggers the next one out, and so on. These seven frames are seven veils, veiling – and in the process of reading, unveiling – the naked beauty of Helen, desired by all men on earth. Yet the seven frames also frame her husband Menelaus's loss of identity as he increasingly has to share Helen's beauty; and as such they tell the story of that loss. Thus the story of Menelaus's loss of self becomes the substitute for that loss.

Menelaus is the legendary cuckold; and Helen is unfaithful to him because his inferiority complex prevents him from believing what Proteus, the seer, tells him: "Helen chose you without reason because she loves you without cause" (*LF*, p. 156). From his wedding night up to present narrative time, Menelaus wants to know why Helen chose him in preference to all the other much more heroic heroes of Greece. Her love cannot satisfy him, since it defies explanation. Baffled, Menelaus begins to tell his story, searching for the flaw in his life that will render the understanding which beauty fails to offer. Since beauty is self-contained, it cannot be understood; the desire for knowledge develops from a deficiency. Beauty is divine, the search for knowledge human. Demigoddess by birth, Helen wanted Menelaus to overcome the gap between divinity and humanity, eternal beauty and its Platonic reflection, through love. Menelaus fails, since he is nothing but human. Helen avenges herself by remaining eternally beautiful, eternally desirable, and, for Menelaus, eternally unattainable. Yet for

Helen to avenge herself eternally, Menelaus too must be made eternal. He becomes immortal through narration, becoming the voice that tells his life-story. Substituting narration for life, Menelaus acquires the role of eternal husband: eternally cuckolded, eternally loved. Yet love, no longer being the substance of life, is consequently transformed into "the absurd, unending *possibility* of love" (*LF*, p. 162; my italics); and only as such can it be told. Loss of identity is the price Menelaus pays for existing in a legend and as a legend. For what a legend ultimately wants to trace is the origin, the truth; yet, it owes its very existence to the fact that the truth recedes before it. If it were able to find the origin, its own reason for being would cease. Only the possibility of the truth of the legend of Menelaus and Helen can be affirmed, and this possibility is once more substantiated by Barth's "Menelaiad" which frames the original story.

Finally "Anonymiad," the last fiction of *Lost in the Funhouse*, is the culmination of Barth's idea of mythical origin as a riddle about the loss of identity which spawns necessary fictions — as interpretations of, and strategies of compensating for, that loss. "Anonymiad" is the story of the nameless minstrel mentioned in Book III of Homer's *Odyssey*, whom Agamemnon left behind to guard Clytemnestra's virtue while he himself went off to fight Troy. Marooned on a desolate island by Clytemnestra's lover Aegisthus, the minstrel is left to himself, not only to lament his fate, brought about by his own false ambition to see the world, but also to transcend the limitations of his ego. He invents the written word and all the literary genres. He then puts his fictions afloat in nine amphorae which Aegisthus has left behind and which, because of the inspiration afforded him by the wine they held, he has named for the nine Muses. At the end of his life the minstrel, who has forgotten his own name during the seven years of his isolation, composes the autobiographical "Anonymiad," a tale not of *an* artist, but of *the* artist:

Seven parts plus head- and tail-piece: the years of my maroonment framed by its causes and prognosis. The prologue was to've established . . . the ground-conceit and the narrative voice and viewpoint: a minstrel stuck on some Aegean clinker commences his story, in the process characterizing himself and hinting at the circumstances leading to his plight. Parts One through Four were to rehearse those circumstances, Five through Seven the stages of his island life vis-à-vis his minstrelling – innocent garrulity, numb silence, and terse self-knowledge, respectively – and fetch the narrative's present time up to the narrator's. The epilogue's a sort of envoi to whatever eyes, against all odds, may one day read it. (*LF*, p. 172)

The image of the artist filling the bellies of his beloved muses with fictions and sending them off into the Aegean links up with the opening stories of *Lost in the Funhouse*, in which the sperm that is to generate the future artist is carried towards the shores of love ("Night-Sea Journey") and the future artist receives a message in a bottle revealing to him his calling ("Water-Message"). The Moebius strip which frames *Lost in the Funhouse* has come full circle. The sperm bearing the artist becomes the drifting amphorae bearing art. The relationship between the author and his fiction has become as unmediated as that between a father and his sperm. The figure of a narrator has become superfluous, because the narrator has lost his ontological justification as a mediator between reality and fiction. Thus *Lost in the Funhouse* can be called a *Künstlerroman* in the extreme: not only written *by* an artist *about* the artist, but substituting itself *for* the artist.

In *Lost in the Funhouse* life is gradually consumed by art: Ambrose Mensch grows up not acquiring *Bildung* for life, but becoming an artist. While the narrative experiments that provide the themes of the rest of the stories of *Lost in the Funhouse* – "Autobiography," "Petition," "Title," and "Life-Story" – constitute an artistic identity, they seem to require the sacrifice of Ambrose as a character. Yet if the artist's development destroys his unquestionable and unquestioning identity, then a conscious regression in time might help to recover that identity. Barth uses Homer's myth of the Mycenaean minstrel to demonstrate that the past, if its exact historical moment and locale are indefinable, dissolves the borderline between reality

55

and fiction, and between identity and anonymity. The anonymous minstrel of the last story in *Lost in the Funhouse* returns story as such to become the watery protoplasm of the first, and artistic solitude bears eventual seed in the drift of time. Here, in new stories generated from old stories in the procreative mystery of love, is the interpretative quality of story which Barth celebrates as essential for life.

*

If *Lost in the Funhouse* seeks the origin of story and finds it above all in myth, which dissolves the borderline between fiction and reality, then Barth's next book, *Chimera*, suggests that this borderline can be transgressed in both directions; fiction can replace life, life can also replace fiction. *Chimera* consists of three novellas, "Dunyazadiad," "Perseid," and "Bellerophoniad," all drawing on mythic roots of narrative. The impact and arrangement of these three novellas are made to resemble the mythical Chimaera — a fire-breathing monster with a lion's head, goat's body, and serpent's tail. But since this Chimaera is in the Bellerophon myth and only appears in the "Bellerophoniad" when Iobates, King of Lycia, sets Bellerophon the task of destroying the monster, this suggests that the stories have a cumulative direction, with the story of the life and death of Bellerophon as the center. And in this story, as in the others, the mythic world of the past is intruded upon from the future world of "reality." The stories of the past do not merely float onward into the future; they can take in a content from that future.

So, at the mid-point of his life, Barth's Bellerophon receives a "water-message" from the future — a letter whose author he supposes to be the seer Polyeidus, the shape-shifter, his mentor, and, as he finally comes to know, his true father. Yet this letter describes the attempt of one Jerome Bonaparte Bray (a descendant of Napoleon's brother Jerome and his American wife Betsy Patterson, and also of Harold Bray, George Giles's adversary in *Giles Goat-Boy*) to compose a "revolutionary" novel called *NOTES* with the aid of a computer. (The reader will learn more of Jerome Bray in Barth's next novel which is called, not quite *NOTES*, but *LETTERS*.) Bellerophon suspects that this computer may be some future version of the seer in his own life. He thus unconsciously foresees Polyeidus's actual relationship to him, for, as a Barth reader would know, the notion of the computer as father has already been established in *Giles Goat-Boy*. As for the concept of the revolutionary novel *NOTES*, it is remarkable in two respects:

> On the one hand, inasmuch as "character," "plot," and for that matter "content," "subject," and "meaning," are attributes of particular novels, the Revolutionary Novel *NOTES* is to dispense with all of them in order to transcend the limitations of particularity; . . . it will represent nothing beyond itself, have no content except its own form, no subject but its own processes. . . . On the other hand, at its "*Phi*-point" . . . there is to occur a single anecdote, a perfect model of a text-within-the-text, a microcosm or paradigm of the work as a whole: . . . "a history of the Greek mythic hero Bellerophon." (*CH*, p. 266)

Chimera is not, nor does it represent, the revolutionary novel *NOTES*. But it reflects upon the conditions of such a novel. It consists of *notes* towards such a novel. And it demonstrates how the story of the Greek mythic hero Bellerophon can serve as a "perfect model of a text-within-the-text," for the story of Bellerophon is "framed" by the story of his cousin Perseus as recounted in the "Perseid." Throughout his life Bellerophon has only copied the heroic life led by his cousin. Perseus has established the pattern on which he feels he must mold himself in order to become a mythic hero; when he leaves Corinth for the world of adventure, he actually asks Polyeidus "for a copy of the Pattern, by way of autobiographical road map" (*CH*, p. 175).

Perseus, at the mid-point of *his* life, had made up his mind to retrace his steps, to repeat his former heroic deeds – beheading the Medusa, liberating Andromeda, petrifying the inimical wedding-guests with Medusa's head – but he wanted to repeat them self-consciously. Thus, the mode of operation during his second enterprise had to be contrary to the first: he had to permit things to happen to him instead of adventuring to them – in order to be able to reflect upon them. Perseus's ironic but nevertheless heroic endeavor is rewarded by the gods: Athene revives Medusa and even restores her original beauty on condition that she does not show her face to anyone. However, there is one escape clause. Medusa is granted the power to rejuvenate or depetrify, just once, whomever she gazes upon or whoever gazes upon her if this person truly loves her. When Perseus finally decides to lift Medusa's veil, their look of mutual love "estellates" them. They become the constellation of Perseus and Medusa. Immortalized, they tell their story to each other every night – "as long as men and women read the stars" (*CH*, p. 142).

Bellerophon contrives to make his life follow a similar path, since Polyeidus has indeed provided him with the Barthian Pattern of Mythic Heroism. He also attempts to create a second cycle of his life, like Perseus devising it as a self-conscious repetition of the first. The double irony of *his* ironic endeavor is that the first cycle of Perseus's life was spontaneous, whereas Bellerophon's own has been a self-conscious imitation from the beginning. He leaves behind his gentle wife and family as well as the kingdom of Lycia, which is prosperous and politically stable, for the sole reason that "because mythic heroes at that age and stage should become the opposite of content, my contentment made me wretched" (*CH*, p. 149). Bellerophon's defect is obvious: he has never been an authentic hero. Since he strives to fulfill the demands of the heroic myth as *story*, his heroism is always belated. This predicament is mirrored in the structure of Barth's book: as Bellerophon's life-story is placed last, it is doomed always to be read *after* that of Perseus – whereas in ancient myth their heroic careers overlapped, Bellerophon thus being granted as much authenticity as Perseus. Thus, all the events in the life of Barth's Bellerophon also have the form of stories; they never appear as a series of heroic deeds that later became the content of a story. Bellerophon's killing of the Chimaera, for instance, is a fiction prescribed for him by Polyeidus. Polyeidus has prepared a special spear which, instead of a sharp bronze point, has a dull lead one, like a pencil. Bellerophon thrusts this spear into the Chimaera's cave. She attacks it and dies when the lead, melted by her fiery breath, burns through her vitals and kills her. Therefore, it is through a trick that the monster dies; it is also a fiction that Bellerophon killed her.

In the same way, the whole life of Barth's Bellerophon is a fiction or lie. Polyeidus, the trickster, manages to make everybody, including Bellerophon himself, believe that Bellerophon is a demigod and that Poseidon is his father, although Polyeidus knows Bellerophon to be supposititious. Bellerophon supposes that he must be a true hero when he is nothing but the hero of Polyeidus's, his father or author's, fiction. Therefore Bellerophon, although he believes he is truly a demigod, does not act like one, but rather like someone interested in the implications of being a demigod – in other words, rather more like an artist than a hero. When Anteia, the sister of his future wife Philonoë, attempts to seduce him, because she wants to become the mother of a demigod, Bellerophon cautiously points out to her how unlikely it is that she will get what she wants from him. With the help of a Mendel diagram he demonstrates to her that since he is a demigod and she is a mortal, they might indeed produce a demigod together but the chances are two to one against it. The probability is reduced considerably by taking into account that the child may be female, that a demigod's embrace, unlike a god's, may fail to impregnate, and that the equal distribution of divine and human sperm is by no means guaranteed. He further goes on to explain to impatient Anteia that personally he would be much more interested in making love to a demigoddess, because a demigod and a demigoddess can do together something that Zeus himself, with a mortal mate, cannot do: produce a full-blooded deity.

> "That's also the only instance of genetical up-breeding in this scheme of possibilities – a child superior by nature to both parents – and the same pairing holds the only possibility of true *down*-breeding. Neither of these hypothetical possibilities, to my knowledge, has been realized in mythic history, but they make the coupling of a demigoddess and myself, for example, a good deal richer in geneticodramatic potential than the coupling of you and me, don't you think?" (*CH*, pp. 191–2)

After this lecture Anteia flees, avenging herself by accusing Bellerophon of the rape which she had hoped for in vain. The comedy here is not superficial; nor is Bellerophon simply trying to avoid making love to Anteia by ruminating on up-breeding and how to create an immortal. Instead he represents the ironic dilemma of the postmodernist author.

This dilemma is implied in the fact that he needs to apply Mendel's nineteenth-century law to the ancient myth of the birth of the hero – that he needs to historicize the mythic time sequence whereby a myth accumulates meaning through mere repetition, in order to justify his claim to heroism. Analogously, the postmodernist author can no longer be an authentic artist; his only claim to originality lies in the reflection upon this dilemma from his own point of view. However, looking backward may yet defy belatedness. As the letter from the future in the "Bellerophoniad" illustrates, the method of applying future results of historic or scientific research to ancient myth can shed new light on patterns that seemed to be exhausted long ago: "Neither of these hypothetical possibilities, to my knowledge, has been realized in mythic history," says Bellerophon. This insight is Bellerophon's – and Barth's – original contribution to mythic history.

Being no demigod, Bellerophon cannot *act* like a mythic hero. Yet as an artist he understands that the immortality achieved through heroic deeds – fame – can to some degree be won by procuring an audience for one's *stories*. Consequently, Bellerophon craves audiences: he constantly tells the tale of how he rode Pegasus and killed the Chimaera to his wife and children, who now know it by heart; at the same time he also tells it to his young Amazon lover Melanippe, who plays to him the role Medusa played to Perseus; finally, it is told to the reader, since at the end of Bellerophon's life Polyeidus changes himself into "you-in-*Bellerophoniad*-form" (*CH*, p. 319). Since Bellerophon is conscious of his craving for an audience, the effects of his stories upon others become a part of those very stories in the retelling. Thus teller and audience become mutually dependent. Similarly, for Bellerophon Perseus's heroic deeds have already become his own myths; he listens to those myths, and his own imitations of Perseus's deeds represent the writer's adaptation of earlier stories. Forgoing his own identity by willingly identifying with his hero, Bellerophon achieves another identity, paradoxical in that it is neither his nor Perseus's, but that of an artist. Though forgoing the dialogue with others which could have established a substitute identity by constantly telling his story, Bellerophon the unsuccessful hero becomes Bellerophon the successful author, partaking of the precarious immortality of the written word: "Loosed at last from mortal speech, he turned into written words: Bellerophonic letters afloat between two worlds, forever betraying, in combinations and recombinations, the man they forever represent" (*CH*, pp. 145–6). Bellerophon's immortality is the result of the constant betrayal of the possibility of undivided presence. Thus he no longer remembers to whom he is telling his story at precisely this moment; he often repeats himself, attempting to fill in possible lacunae for a particular audience. This process whereby the author loses himself in the text could only be brought to a halt if the story were always addressed to the same, ideal audience.

The postmodernist author's need for an ideal reader is the theme of the first novella in *Chimera*, "Dunyazadiad," which retells the story of Scheherazade telling the stories of *The Thousand and One Nights*. Tradition has it that by beguiling King Shahryar with the infolded stories she relates, she saves her life over a thousand and one nights. The King's threatening power denies him the role of ideal audience (Barth has said that Shahryar represents the male-chauvinist extreme of the American academic "publish or perish" principle), but Scheherazade *is* the ideal story-teller, for she translates an existentially suspensive situation into a dramatic suspension of disbelief which, in turn, prevents her death. Moreover, her transfer of continuous peril into narrative resourcefulness intrigues the subsequent reader or listener. The King becomes a secondary figure; the listener or reader who can appreciate this transformation becomes the ideal audience. The ideal listener is represented in Dunyazade, Scheherazade's little sister, who each night initiates her telling of a new story or instigates the continuation of a story-in-progress, each time creating the situation in which story-telling can occur. The ideal reader is

61

represented by John Barth himself, who offers himself as the inspiration of the artist, being able to transport himself back into Scheherazade's times after having accidentally written down the words: "The key to the treasure is the treasure" (*CH*, p. 19) – the very words Scheherazade speaks when desperate about how to deal with a king who deflowers a virgin each night and kills her in the morning. So she is shown to be overwhelmed when John Barth, "The Genie" from the future, offers to tell her one of the stories collected in *The Thousand and One Nights* every day so that she can then tell it to the King at night. Scheherazade had once had the idea of charming the King with stories herself, but had abandoned it as impractical. She now regains confidence in this device from the proof, provided by The Genie, that it will really work. John Barth, the ideal reader, thus creates the ideal story-teller; but, more importantly, he proves the advantage of the written over the spoken word, since it is the text, preserved through centuries, that unlocks the treasure of the past.

The interpretation of the novella hinges on the words: the key to the treasure *is* the treasure. They are magic words, because it appears as if Barth and Scheherazade were thinking of them at the same time when in fact centuries separate them. Transporting himself back into Scheherazade's time, Barth can meet her as if they were two people alive at the same time. Yet they also meet as author and reader meet – through an act of the imagination. Finally, they meet as potential lovers since they agree "that writing and reading, or telling and listening, were literally ways of making love" (*CH*, p. 32). What Barth means to demonstrate with the magic tryst between the Author and Scheherazade is the actual value of what he calls heartfelt possibilities. His endeavor in *Chimera* is to present the importance of story-telling (and love) in the face of ultimate extinction – the end of the story ("Dunyazadiad"), the end of life ("Bellerophoniad"), the end of man ("Perseid").

"The key to the treasure *is* the treasure" means that truth is more likely to be found in possibility than in reality. Just as Bellerophon's life proved to be a lie, Scheherazade's stories prove to be true; or, in Barth's words: "They're too important to be lies. Fictions, maybe – but truer than fact" (*CH*, p. 61).

The importance of her stories or fictions is made manifest through their longevity. If, after centuries, John Barth can still be enchanted by Scheherazade's stories-within-her-story to the degree that he needs to express his "lifelong adoration" (*CH*, p. 20) of her through a series of written homages like the present novella, then her story as well as her stories have proved to be truer than her possible life and death.[9] The *Künstlerroman* has superseded the artist. Not only has the artist been made superfluous, as in the end of *Lost in the Funhouse*, but in *Chimera* the artist's life-story merely frames the truth which his artistic inspiration has conjured up as if by magic.

5

THE SUPRA-REALISTIC NOVEL:
"LETTERS" AND "SABBATICAL"

After having successfully refined the artist out of existence at the end of *Chimera*, Barth faced a fresh paradox: since the narrative now presented itself as objective, the author's subjective voice could only be a fiction. In *LETTERS* (1979) the "capital-A Author," seeking moral support, writes letters to several of his former fictional characters as well as to his muse, the personification of literary history, in order to solicit epistolary responses from them. These, together with his own letters, constitute the novel. Barth appeals to (literary) history – his own as well as others' – in order to regain a foothold in reality. As Author he grants his characters more "real" independence than they had in his earlier fictions (he appears to be interested in the opinions they have formed in the meantime), while at the same time raising *LETTERS* to the level of metafiction or the second degree of fictionality.[10] Thus Barth moves away from traditional narrative in two directions: the *Author* claims to be a character among other characters, making the degree of the characters' familiarity to readers of Barth more important than their fictionality; and since a metafiction has as one topic its own fictionality, the *author* appears to be reflecting upon rather than creating a narrative. The narrative, or plot, seems to create itself – objectively.

LETTERS: an old time epistolary novel by seven fictitious drolls & dreamers, each of which imagines himself actual. They will write always in this order: Lady Amherst, Todd Andrews, Jacob Horner, A. B. Cook, Jerome Bray, Ambrose Mensch, the Author. Their letters will total 88 . . . divided unequally into seven sections according to a certain scheme. . . . Their several narratives will become one; like waves of a rising tide, the plot will surge forward, recede, surge farther forward, recede less far, et cetera to its climax and dénouement.

On with the story. (*L*, p. 49)

The reader is in the same role as the Author's addressees in that he reads the letters Barth has written (the Author's as well as the characters') and his response could be analogous to that of any of the Author's correspondents. Yet, since he is only an observer, he is forced into the role of critic, becoming as remote from the plot as the author himself, so that he receives an objective description of the novel's structure, authorial presuppositions, and intent.

The typography of the title is itself an example of the novel's self-reflexivity. The capital letters of *LETTERS* relate to the capital-A Author who collects the letters of his "readers" or characters (whereas the author presents this collection of letters to his "critic" or reader). Also, the word *LETTERS* is not printed as one would expect on a title page. Instead, each letter of the word *LETTERS* consists of miniature letters which, if read consecutively, spell out the explanatory subtitle of the novel. This subtitle, "an old time epistolary novel by seven fictitious drolls & dreamers, each of which imagines himself actual," relates to the title as *signifiant* relates to *signifié*. However, since both are folded into the word *LET-TERS*, the gap between signifier and signified, indicative of the rupture between reality and language, can be successfully bridged by the self-referential text. Both title and subtitle, in capital and small letters, thus sum up what the novel is about, although appearing only to ascribe *LETTERS* to an historical genre ("an old time epistolary novel") and describe the letter writers ("seven . . . drolls & dreamers"). The subtitle calls into question the ontological status of these seven "authors," the possibility of ultimately defining the realm of their existence ("seven *fictitious* drolls & dreamers, each of which imagines himself *actual*"); and since ambiguous authorship undermines the authenticity of any text, but especially of a letter, the subtitle calls into question the genre it names, the "epistolary novel." The seven "authors" are called "drolls & dreamers" because they seem to be mistaken in assuming their own actuality. They write letters as if to real persons, although they exist only in a novel. However, the question of actuality or fictitiousness not only pertains to the seven letter writers, but also to the author. Since titles of fictions are not necessarily part of the narrative, it is uncertain whether "drolls & dreamers" has to be seen as a label bestowed upon the letter writers by the Author or as an ironic self-indictment of the author, originating in a self-awareness of his own ambiguous ontological status. The author is aware of the fact that he exists as fictional as well as actual author and is responsible for his characters' uncertain self-awareness. Hoping to unburden himself of this responsibility, he has recourse to a higher authority, the muse.

However, the self-reflexive twentieth-century author has to create his own muse. Lady Amherst, Barth's muse in *LETTERS*, is one of his letter writers. In her role as Muse she starts off each of the seven sections of the book. She also advances the plot through the description of her encounters with each of the other letter writers. All of these encounters are "actual" within the borderlines of the text, particularly her love affair with Ambrose Mensch, John Barth's *alter ego*, whose youthful aspirations to the writing profession the reader knows from *Lost in the Funhouse*. The only person whom Lady Amherst does not encounter in person is the Author himself, to whom all her letters are addressed. But since the author rids himself of his *alter ego* at the end of the novel, exorcising his former fictional self, so to speak, a union of Author and Muse ultimately becomes a real possibility in that they generate *LETTERS* together. At the beginning of the novel Lady Amherst, in her function as acting provost of the Faculty of Letters of Marshyhope State University College in Dorchester, Maryland, writes to John Barth, inviting him to accept from that institution the honorary degree of Doctor of Letters. She adds a long postscript to the formal invitation, explaining the politics of the university and her own role in those politics as well as that of Ambrose Mensch, and pleads with the Author to accept the invitation. The final sentence of the postscript reads:

> Do therefore respond at your earliest to this passing odd epistle, whose tail like the spermatozoon's far outmeasures its body, the better to accomplish its single urgent end, and — like Molly Bloom at the close of *her* great soliloquy (whose author was, yes, a friend of your friend's friend) — say to us *yes*, to the Litt. D. *yes*, to MSU *yes*, and *yes* Dorchester, *yes* Tidewater, Maryland *yes yes yes!* (*L*, pp. 11–12)

This final sentence reveals her identity — to the Author as well as to the reader. Lady Amherst, of British descent, in her mid-forties at the time she writes this letter, dated 8 March 1969, is the personification of modernist literature or rather, since she has known most of the great modernist writers, some of them intimately, the personification of the history of that literary movement. She can thus become the muse for the post-modernist writer, for whom modernism as a literary tradition is the source of inspiration, notwithstanding the fact that modernist literature is something against which he needs to rebel, whose representative he will not "meet," in order to define himself as a writer. Lady Amherst's comparison of herself with Molly Bloom indicates her literalness as well as her literacy — that is, she assumes the role of Molly Bloom while at the same time reflecting upon that role. She says *yes* to Barth's *alter ego* Ambrose Mensch in the same literal sense in which Molly Bloom said yes to *her* husband-to-be. And she says *yes* to the Author John Barth by inviting him to say *yes* to her as his postmodernist American — Maryland — muse. (Her reference also seems to hint at a reversal of modernism through post-modernism by referring to the tail of the sperm cell, a motif from "Night-Sea Journey," the first of the fictions of *Lost in the Funhouse* which, like this letter, starts off the novel, whereas one would expect "tail" to refer to an end, like Molly Bloom's soliloquy at the end of *Ulysses*.) The love relationship between Ambrose Mensch and Lady Amherst produces a child, a configuration mirrored in the union of modernism (Lady Amherst) and postmodernism (John Barth), the outcome of which is *LETTERS*.

The understanding of the novel hinges on the qualities or connotations of the word *letters*. Towards the end of the book the Author, in a letter to Ambrose Mensch – that is in a sense to himself – explains the project of *LETTERS*, as yet only conceived and still to develop in his mind:

> Here's what I know about the book so far. Its working title is *LETTERS*. It will consist of letters (like this, but with a plot) between several correspondents, the capital-A Author perhaps included, and preoccupy itself with, among other things, the role of epistles – real letters, forged and doctored letters – in the history of History. It will also be concerned with, and of course constituted of, alphabetical letters: the atoms of which the written universe is made. Finally, to a small extent the book is addressed to the phenomenon of literature itself, the third main sense of our word *letters*. (*L*, p. 654)

Despite the earlier protestations by the Author that the epistolary novel had already been worked to death by the end of the eighteenth century and that he blushes to report his present fascination with the genre, the author derives the working principle of the book from the time gap between the eighteenth and the twentieth centuries. Letters can be "forged" or "doctored" only because every letter has two times, that of its writing and that of its reading. The change of meaning takes place during the interim between the conception and the reception of a letter. Both the writer and the reader of the letter are deceived, the "forger" or "doctorer" playing upon the ignorance or innocence of both. Fiction, or the play of the imagination, is a similar "deception," developing as it does in the interstices between real, or historic, events. John Barth declines Lady Amherst's offer of an honorary degree of "Doctor of Letters" for good reasons. The Author prefers not to be called a doctorer or forger of letters, because the meaning of the text – like that of a letter – may change in the period between its conception and its reception. Time itself is the "Doctor of Letters." The author cannot decide whether to favor life over art or art over life, the actual but restricted reality of the writer and the reader or the deceptive but also suggestive realm of fiction. Instead, he projects the arguments concerning the relationship between "life" and "art"[11] upon his characters, testing through them a variety of possible attitudes.

The character in Barth's fiction who is most given to the manipulation of history in the interstices of reality is Henry Burlingame III in *The Sot-Weed Factor*, whose innocent counterpart is Ebenezer Cooke. Henry Burlingame eventually had a child with Anna, Ebenezer Cooke's twin sister, and the two lineages began to intertwine. On page 112 of *LETTERS* Barth presents the reader with a genealogical chart of the Cook(e)/Burlingame families, which reveals that the descendants were in turn named Cooke Burlingame or Burlingame Cook. One of those descendants, Andrew Burlingame Cook IV, whose letters are quoted by one of the seven letter writers, describes to his unborn child the interdependence between the Cooks and Burlingames:

> Child: I am a Cook, not a Burlingame. You Burlingames get from your ancestor H. B. III a passion for the world that fetches you everywhere at once, in guises manifold as the world's, to lead & shape its leaders & shapers. We Cooks, I know now, get from our forebear Ebenezer, the virgin poet of Maryland, an inexhaustible innocence that, whatever our involvement in the world . . . inclines us to be followers — better, learners: tutees of the Burlingames & those they've shaped. (*L*, p. 312)

Andrew Burlingame Cook IV is quoted by his great-great-grandson, Andrew Burlingame Cook VI, like Ebenezer Cooke laureate of Maryland — and another phony laureate to boot. The existence and emergence in *LETTERS* of the four letters of A. B. Cook IV, which end on the eve of the War of 1812, are part of the legacy of his great-great-grandson, A. B. Cook VI, who regards himself as Barth's collaborator on the *LETTERS* project. However, it is important to note that the two sets of letters are as far apart in time as the "death" of the epistolary novel and Barth's revivification of the genre. This seeming coincidence points to the fact that history and literature may both have been doctored or forged in the time that has elapsed between the past and the present. The letters of A. B. Cook IV, addressed to "his unborn child," who will turn out to be twins, reveal how the Cook(e)/Burlingame families always tried to tamper with American history, and the ambivalent ontological status of letters in general further facilitates such tampering – as exemplified by the "historical" letters constituting another as yet "unborn child": *LETTERS*.

Historians tend to interpret letters as documents. They believe that even texts which are admittedly informed by a personal point of view can yield factual results if analyzed objectively. *LETTERS* defies that notion. For Barth the results of such analysis would still be subject to historical change in that they could be reinterpreted in a different fashion. History for Barth is not a nightmare from which he is trying to awake, as it is for Stephen Dedalus in *Ulysses*; it is not a prison house of ineluctable facts. Instead, it can give rise to a philosophy of the possible. Stephen Dedalus asks himself whether the facts of history as we know them may not have precluded all other possibilities, since those other possibilities never were. Thus only that could have been possible which eventually came to pass. Since Caesar was stabbed to death, he could not have died differently.[12] For Barth, the facts of history are not the corollary of their possibility, as for Joyce, but rather the premise of other possibilities. They seem to be like texts that allow for various interpretations. However, that is not to say that Barth substitutes textuality or intertextuality for factuality. Decisive, for him, is the time span between past and present. A genuine letter, written at a given historical time and describing the political events of that time, will be nothing but a subjective account of those events. Even if this letter survives the passage of time, only its factual existence will gain in importance, while the events themselves gradually lose whatever ontological relevance they once possessed. On the other hand, a fictive letter that describes past events will make those events appear more factual. Thus Barth's (or his characters') present version of past events may become more important – more "real" – than an historical account of those events.

In those four letters to his unborn child, A. B. Cook IV explains the family's involvement with history as a concern with origins – history as genealogy. For instance, he reveals two cases of intermarriage with Indian princesses from the tribes of the Ahatchwhoops and the Tarratines that led to the family's participation in the Indian uprisings under the leadership of Pontiac and Tecumseh.[13] He also discloses the involvement, particularly of the male members of the family, with European and Europe-orientated American history between the Revolutionary War and the War of 1812, the latter being for Cook IV the second American revolution. Barth's strategy in *LETTERS* is to show that, if chance had operated differently, all the well-known events of the American Revolution (which would be celebrated during the Bicentennial in 1976, the year of the scheduled publication of Barth's novel) might have had a different outcome. Indeed, it appears as if deviations from the received historical facts would have been all but unavoidable if each generation of Cooks and Burlingames had not, in an act of filial revolt, cancelled out their respective forebears' achievements and thus ultimately served to nullify the family's impact on American history. From the point of view of *LETTERS*, the second American revolution was no true revolution, but a re-enactment of the first, a tragic farce, as such acquiring literary rather than literal importance. Therefore, A. B. Cook IV's fictional letters become more important than the events they describe.

In rewriting history, Barth does not change a single detail of what has been handed down. However, he has rewritten history as History, as a series of fictional plots or intrigues that should have happened, but that counterbalance one another to the point where they have no apparent effect on the course of actual historical events. Thus he can set ineffectual public action against the efficacy of the private imagination, culminating in the sometimes prophetic quality of private dreams. In a letter "To Whom It May Concern" the Author describes "three concentric dreams of waking." In the first, on waking half-entranced from a siesta in the Dorchester marshes, he imagines himself a Rip Van Winkle-like narrator who lived the first half of his life from 1776 to 1812, and the second half from 1940 to 1976 — with a sleep of 128 years in between. He feels for an imaginary silver pocket watch with his father's monogram HB (Henry Burlingame?) before looking at his wristwatch. Bees

71

buzz around him, and he reflects upon the significance of the letter (or initial) B, the cabalist's letter for Creation. (Even if B and H, the first and last letters of Barth's name, were "lost," that is if the boundaries of the Author's present state were dissolved as in a dream, then "art" would remain.) During his second dream of waking, the impressions from his first dream are organized into patterns that will influence the organization of *LETTERS*. The significance of the bees becomes apparent in the relationship between Jerome Bray and Bea Golden, the queen of the beehive that is his computer, or in the name and mellifluousness of the Author's *alter ego*, Ambrose Mensch, whose naming after a swarm of bees that settled on him was recorded earlier in "Ambrose His Mark," one of the fictions of *Lost in the Funhouse*. Marshes too are significant for a Maryland author and, since reed pens and papyri were the first tools used in writing, for an author in general. In the last concentric dream these patterns then evolve into the elements of the novel itself, just as the letter that describes the three dreams has become a part of it.

The crucial question is which of the three dreams represents the innermost of the three concentric circles: the first, "realistic," dream, or the last, "fictional," dream of a novel called *LETTERS* which the reader, the one concerned, finds before him? Does a real experience expand to generate a fictional text, or does the structure of a text call for a reality to match it? The author himself calls his fiction "not autobiographic but mildly prophetic" (*L*, p. 48). As an example he cites the fact that after his decision, in 1968, that the "Author" in his novel would be offered an honorary doctorate of letters from a Maryland university, he received in 1969, the date of Lady Amherst's letter, just such an invitation in the mail. The point in question here is not whether dreams can come true, but whether dreams represent a realm where fiction and reality become indistinguishable. Just as letters have two times, that of their writing and that of their reading, and just as every letter is written with a view to its being read, that is with a view to the future, while it is always read with a view to the past, that is with a view to the original intention of the author, the dream is also concerned with the past and the future. Dream can be defined as a gap in

72

the experienced continuity of the present. It deals with the facts of the past as if they were future adventures. Thus it opens up possibilities for the human imagination in the space created by sleep (here prolonged as in Rip Van Winkle's case) so that the Author, as in the second (central?) dream, can develop patterns that will apply both to reality and to fiction.

To set off his own notion of dreams, the author introduces as one of the seven letter writers Jacob Horner, the protagonist of *The End of the Road*, who is asked by Joseph Morgan to redream history and bring Rennie, his dead wife, back to life. In a *Wiedertraum*, a restaging of past events with substitute dramatis personae where necessary, Jacob Horner attempts to atone for and thus overcome his own past. During the crucial scene, the re-enactment of Rennie's seduction, he reverses the plot by offering his new bride, Marsha Blank, former wife of Ambrose Mensch, to Joseph Morgan as a form of recompense for his own former trespasses. Joseph Morgan accepts, actually "fills in the blank" – in contrast to Ambrose's merely imaginative attempt in *Lost in the Funhouse* to fill in the blank of the water-message he receives – and thus loses his hold on his adversary, which consisted of his belief that the order of facts is immutable since it can be accounted for through human rationality. Understanding that rationality has lost the battle to irrationality, Joe shoots himself. The redreaming of his own history ends Jacob Horner's immobility; it functions as therapy. Yet it is not an act of the imagination. It was prescribed by Joseph Morgan, and its surprise ending is but a logical reversal of Joe's demand – which he all but expected. Jacob Horner thus not only reveals his own limitations, but points to the novel's central authorial presupposition.

All the letter writers in *LETTERS* – with the exception of Lady Amherst – are limiting cases with regard to the Author, since each of the characters represents but one aspect of the author, making that aspect absolute. None can therefore escape the vicissitudes inherent in following any one principle too rigorously. Even Ambrose Mensch, who in the fashion of the mythical hero Perseus from *Chimera* (Ambrose is supposed to have written the "Perseid"), attempts to re-enact the earlier stages of his life in order to transcend his former limitations, ultimately must defer to Lady Amherst's love and her sense of self-irony. This one-sidedness of the "authors" of LETTERS might seem to inhibit the development of the Author's imagination. As characters, they represent the narrative resistance offered by others to the unlimited exfoliation of a central intelligence and sensibility. The Author has to take them into consideration, just as a letter writer has to consider the expectations of the recipients of his letters. At the same time, however, these characters are the author's, if not the Author's, own creations. He has lifted them out of his earlier fictions; so that the characters' limitations are only those of the former stages of his own imaginative development. By bringing representatives of different developmental stages of his imagination together within one book, the author erases those stages, and develops the characters' attitudes into contemporaneous facets of his present, Author's, consciousness.

LETTERS deals with epistles or letters. It also deals with alphabetical letters: "the atoms of which the written universe is made." The book is divided into seven sections, lettered, instead of numbered, as follows: L, E, T, T, E, R and S. Each of these letters appears superimposed on one of the calendar pages of the seven months from March through September 1969. This device not only determines the dates of the letters compiled in each of the seven sections, but also the number of letters written by each participant. Again these epistles are lettered, instead of numbered, by letters, which once more spell out the subtitle of the novel: "an old time epistolary novel . . ." As demonstrated by the letters of Jerome Bray, this play on alphabetical letters in the novel is not gratuitous. The superimposition of letters upon the numbers of the calendar pages points to the basic cultural, or ideological, opposition Barth intended to deal with in LETTERS: Literature vs. Numerature.

Jerome Bray, descendant of Jerome Bonaparte, youngest brother of Napoleon Bonaparte, as well as of Harold Bray from Giles Goat-Boy, has a "real" heritage intermingled with a "fictional" heritage. His illustrious ancestors each aspired to greatness in one of those opposite ontological realms, unsuccessfully, however. Consequently, Jerome Bray cannot be sure whether he is a real or a fictional person. In fact, he may be of the order of insects. And just as the fall of the Roman Empire is said by some to have been brought about by the anopheles mosquito from the marshes on which Rome was built, Jerome Bray, Lord of the Bees in the guise of a human bee-ing, wants to bring about the fall of the United States through another revolution. However, he not only plots a "Novel Revolution," but also a "Revolutionary Novel," and he is assisted in this double endeavor by a computer which may be as closely related to the world of insects as is Bray himself. Bray's revolutionary epic aspires to pure form. What this means is hinted at in his invitation to Bea Golden, daughter of (in all likelihood) Todd Andrews from *The Floating Opera*, to star in this revolutionary epic:

> It requires a 1st-magnitude female to play *Regina de Nominatrix* . . . royal consort to *Rex Numerator*. . . . To sit at his right hand at the Table of Multiplication, play Ordinate to his Abscissa, share the Pentagonal Bed, receive his innumerable seed, make royal jelly, and bring forth numerous golden heirs. (*L*, p. 638)

The metaphor here is that of a beehive, as indicated by the name of Bray's chosen consort, Bea Golden, the reference to the Pentagonal Bed, which alludes to the form of a honeycomb (or of the building in Washington upon which a revolutionary attack would have to be made), the royal jelly, and the numerous "golden" heirs (conceived like one of Zeus's, who came upon Danaë in a shower of gold). Bray, the *Rex Numerator*, sees himself as the omnipotent "Author". Yet, as the epithet *Numerator* reveals, his public as well as his private strategies are mathematical and abstract rather than literary and concrete. He asks Bea Golden to sit with him at the "Table of Multiplication" (which may also relate to the hoped-for effects of his "innumerable seed" upon her) and to "play Ordinate to his Abscissa." Since the Cartesian co-ordinate system can be used to define any point P, here the Phi-point at six-sevenths of the way through Bray's Revolutionary Novel (and this letter at approximately six-sevenths of the way through Barth's novel), it can in a sense be said to represent a form of "meta-physics" which would define any "physical" point, just as it does this

75

particular climactic point where Jerome Bray and Bea Golden would meet. Thus the metaphysical element of Bray's composite metaphor – alluded to in phrases like "to sit at his right hand" or in the use of epithets like *Rex* and *Regina* (which usually refer to God and the Virgin Mary) as well as in Bray's "ascent" at the end of *LETTERS* – is used allegorically in order to represent the idea of "meta-physics," or pure form.

Just as Jerome Bray's ancestor Harold Bray was the adversary and the only true challenge to George Giles in *Giles Goat-Boy*, Bray turns out to be Barth's only true rival as a novelist. Although Bray does not represent Barth's fictional *alter ego* as does Ambrose Mensch, he nevertheless challenges Barth the novelist in that he challenges literature as such. ("Bee" also represents the letter B, the letter of Creation. Moreover, Jerome Bray's initials are also the initials of John Barth.) The Author had agreed in an early letter that an ongoing film be made of his "latest" book; Bray, in his invitation to Bea Golden, calls novels and films "obsolescent media, soon to be superseded by coaxial television and laser holography, ultimately by a medium far more revolutionary, its essence the very key to and measure of the universe" (*L*, p. 637). This revolutionary medium must be one which no longer represents or even "is" the message, but which can dispense with the message altogether, because it is – numerature. Our words and our language and therefore our meaningful messages are made up of letters. If with the help of, say, the computer's binary system we could eventually substitute numbers (*NUMBERS* is Bray's title for his Revolutionary Novel and thus the alternate to *LETTERS*) for letters and rethink our world accordingly, then we would only have to structure this world instead of having to interpret it. Metaphors, symbols, and allegories would become obsolete, since they carry a meaning which derives from the tension between irreconcilable signifiers. A comprehensive digital system without letters, or literature, would dissolve this tension.

Barth clearly takes a stand for Literature – against Numerature. He opts for the "real" world as we find it today: a medley of languages, literatures, cultures. Therefore, *LETTERS* is a "realistic" novel. Yet Barth knows that any return to literary realism at this historical juncture is impossible. Since in *LETTERS* he needs to re-employ his former literary strategies along with his former fictional characters, and since even his earlier novels have to be considered as parodies of their respective genre, realism in *LETTERS* has to take the form of an irony of irony, or supra-realism. The device of an "irony of irony" can serve Barth, in the form of dialectic principle, to reconstitute realism — literary realism leading to irony, as irony of irony leads to realism. Thus, "realism" in *LETTERS* is no longer a literary strategy (Barth is not renouncing his insight, voiced in *Lost in the Funhouse*, that realism as a literary mode serves only to enhance an illusion of reality), but rather a means of salvaging our world, particularly our written universe, and defending it against pure form. As Ambrose Mensch says:

> If one imagines an artist less enamored of the world than of the language we signify it with, yet less enamored of the language than of the signifying narration, and yet less enamored of the narration than of its formal arrangement, one need *not* necessarily imagine that artist therefore forsaking the world for language, language for the processes of narration, and those processes for the abstract possibilities of form. (*L*, p. 650)

No realism, however, is devoid of perils, because any acceptance of its implications makes the Author more vulnerable to attacks from reality itself. Therefore, as a form of exorcism of these possible perils, the author has them materialize in the further life of Todd Andrews, his first protagonist and, in a sense, most realistic version of himself. Almost 70 years of age, Todd Andrews eventually succumbs to them. Before, his letters to his dead father continue the Inquiries into his own life as well as into his father's death which he had begun in *The Floating Opera*. Like Ambrose Mensch, Todd also attempts to recycle his life; yet his ironic re-enactment of former events rests on nothing but a formal reversal of the values he had held earlier. Todd does not call into question and then re-evaluate value systems as such. His form of re-enactment is not ironic in the sense that Ambrose's re-enactment is ironic. Ambrose attempts to transcend moral strictures for the sake of the freedom of the

77

imagination – by attempting to get Lady Amherst, that is literary history, pregnant with his own creation. Whereas in *The Floating Opera* Todd believed that "nothing has intrinsic value," he has now begun to feel "that Nothing *has* intrinsic value ... which is as much as to say: *Everything* has intrinsic value!" (*L*, p. 96). This new attitude leads Todd to an unconditional acceptance of life instead of an attempt to reject it, as in *The Floating Opera*. However, the assumption that everything has intrinsic value precludes the possibility of establishing priorities in one's life. Thus, Todd remains incapable of making choices. Politically, he is a liberal; philosophically, he holds the Tragic View of things which would leave everything unchanged; emotionally, he can only become involved when he meets with some mode of resistance. His inability to establish priorities ultimately leads to his "existential" death, "mildly" prophesied by his name. Instead of helping his daughter Jeannine lay the foundation for a new, sober life, he rejects her company and, feeling guilty, rapes her. Then he sets about having himself blown up in the "Tower of Truth," thus coming full circle instead of finding a way of life that would integrate re-enactment and development.

For Barth, the propinquity of "realism" and realism is obvious and disturbing. Todd Andrews represents a possibility of exorcising the author's apprehension about his impulse towards realism. He provides the foil against which this realism may, doubly ironic, appear as "realism." For the author's "realism" reflects and rereflects his character's realism – after the author has ironically reflected upon, that is distanced himself from his character as from himself. In so far as all the male characters in *LETTERS* are limiting cases as compared to the author, the novel can be seen as a gigantic exercise in the exorcism of every one of the author's possible limitations. After *LETTERS*, he was left free to explore the imaginative possibilities of supra-realism.

*

The purely "fictional" relationship between the Author and Lady Amherst in *LETTERS* can thus become the "real" relationship between the two story-tellers, one male, the other female, in Barth's next novel, *Sabbatical: A Romance* (1982). The reader is given a symbolic key to this possibility even at the end of *LETTERS*. In a movie wedding scene between Ambrose Mensch and Lady Amherst, the couple is addressed as "Mr & Mrs Key" and presented with the key to the city of Baltimore — and to love. In *Sabbatical* this theme as well as the name Key (for the male protagonist) and the locality are taken up and shifted towards the realm of the author's reality. Yet while the author himself claims that *Sabbatical* is realistic, he nevertheless denies that it is an autobiographical novel.[14] What he seems to mean is that *Sabbatical* is a realistic novel exploring the possibilities of imaginative life. As the subtitle states, the novel is *A Romance*. The term "romance" here refers both to the grotesque romance of mystery and the magical romance of the fairy-tale. For the author, both these imaginative realms serve the primal experiences of life.

As in *LETTERS*, supra-realism in *Sabbatical* derives its justification from the fact that past reality and past fiction cannot be distinguished ontologically, not even where the origin of the characters is concerned. Thus, the story's literary precursors can become its literal ancestors. Edgar Allan Poe is resurrected in the story as Edgar Allan Ho, baby son of Eastwood Ho, a refugee Vietnamese poet. Edgar Allan Ho is Susan's (the protagonist's) nephew, the son of her twin sister Miriam. Susan and Miriam are putative descendants of Poe. The ancestry is a little dubious, given the fact that Poe was childless when he died in Baltimore. But Susan's and Miriam's mother, who represents the capacity for present-day magic in the novel, declares that children are never derived from their immediate progenitors anyway. Thus, Baltimorean Edgar Allan Ho (or his author) might be the truest heir of Edgar Allan Poe, at least in terms of literary genes.

In Poe's fiction, the mysterious and the grotesque are inseparable. The grotesque always implies a distortion of reality; and the mysterious tends to be an undiscovered and, in terms of reality, undiscoverable crime. Similarly, Key Island in Chesapeake Bay, where the two story-tellers Fenwick and Susan anchor after a sudden storm (reminiscent of the "rushing and mighty, but soundless winds" at the end of the *Narrative of*

A. Gordon Pym), cannot be detected on any nautical chart. Perhaps it does not really exist; perhaps it is a training center and hideout for the CIA, where both Fenwick and his recently disappeared twin brother Manfred were formerly employed. Its suggested political importance makes Key Island also reminiscent of Francis Scott Key, author of "The Star-Spangled Banner." Fenwick Scott Key Turner is believed to be a descendant of the author of the national anthem. Fenwick's and Susan's boat is named *Pokey*, after their two famous antecedents, and whenever they return to Baltimore after any prolonged absence, they visit both Fort McHenry and Old Westminster Churchyard where Poe was buried. A literary ancestry is treated by the protagonists as a literal patrimony, requiring physical homage to the material things of the ancestors' domain.

Here the author is not merely having his fictional characters take up the real interests of his life, turning them into art. The relation between character motivation and the events of literary and political history that have influenced the author is again ironic: neither fiction nor history is privileged. In this way, the Author, who represents the narrative point of view of both Fenwick and Susan, once more calls the distinction between art and life into question. And the key that unlocks the mystery of how this distinction can be overcome is the idea of the story. The imagination thus defines the realm where genuine stories of life are told. Fenwick functions as the "turner," playing at the very threshold between art and life:

I see now what we're about. It's the story! . . . It will be our story. What's more . . . this story, our story, it's our house and our child. . . . We'll have made it . . . and we'll live in it. We'll even live by it. It doesn't have to be *about* us – children aren't about their parents. But our love will be in it, and our friendship too. This boat ride will be in it, somehow. It'll be about things coming around to where they started and then going on a little farther in a different way. It should have ancestry in it and offspring; Once upon a time to Happily ever after. (*S*, pp. 356–7)

For Fenwick the challenge is clear: he and Susan want to live, one might even say "perform," a story, a story that is not *about* anyone, does not represent anything by referring to another reality outside itself. In short, Fenwick wants to use the language of story-telling to live in the world, not merely to refer to the things of the world.

Barth has always tried to have it both ways, to tell and live stories. The ambivalent use of language required by Fenwick's enterprise — for he and Susan must appropriate language and yet live through language's revelatory potential — is evidenced in Susan's ethnic mispronunciation of the word "flashback" as "fleshbeck." Susan's *flesh beck*ons to Fenwick, just as female flesh has beckoned to the male ever since Adam and Eve. Susan's transformation of the word, then, establishes a conceptual link between the couple's private conversation, their physical intimacy, and their cultural and biological functions; it relates their private story to all other stories. To establish this link is Susan's privilege, "because flashbacks, Fenwick mildly asserts, may be said to be 'female,' following his notion of forks and confluences: rafting down the stream of time, they retrace what, coming up, were dilemmas, choices, channel-forks" (*S*, p. 173). Thus the female narrative point of view relates to the past, the male to the future, while their conjunction can solve what in the present appears as "dilemmas, choices, channel-forks."

There *are* dilemmas and choices as well as channel-forks that Fenwick and Susan have to face on their extended sabbatical cruise. Fenwick, an aspiring writer who was dismissed by the CIA after having published *Kudove*, an exposé of the agency's Clandestine Services division, is divorced and fifteen years older than his second wife Susan. She is 35, an associate professor of American literature and creative writing at Washington College in Chestertown, Maryland. Fenwick has a cardiac condition (like Todd Andrews in *The Floating Opera*) and wants no more children. Susan is torn between her desire to have children and her ambition to continue her academic career. When she does become pregnant, Susan has an abortion. The Author has Susan discover later that she would have had twins. Thus Fenwick's and Susan's attempt to have a "normal" family life fails. After a visit to their respective families, they return to their boat, presumably to finish their sabbatical cruise.

This is the story line which Fenwick decides to turn into *their* story line – with the story substituting for the child and a permanent home. Fenwick's final discovery – that the story of one's life can be turned into a life-story – has been one of the author's insights ever since *Lost in the Funhouse*. That the author should have Susan and Fenwick employing his own narrative principle suggests not repetition, but a new – "realistic" – structural metaphor, the rise and fall of the tides: the same insight moves up and down between Author and characters, so to speak. On the one hand, the story thus assumes a cyclical pattern; Fenwick's insight at the end of the story is the condition for its beginning. On the other hand, the Author and protagonist(s) become identical; the world becomes "a seamless web" where writing and loving, art and life, cannot be separated or understood in terms of cause and effect. There is a clear allusion here to Poe's narrative of Arthur Gordon Pym, where the question arises of how Pym, in facing the maelstrom at the end of the story, could ever have come to write it in the first place. Unless one assumes that it might have been the interruption of the writing which ended the story, rather than the end of the story which interrupted the writing, there can be no answer. The interruption of the writing of one's life-story can only occur through death. Thus, in order to create a fairy-tale romance, Fenwick and Susan will have to create a cyclical life-story. Susan says, looking at Fenwick: "If that's going to be our story, then let's begin it at the end and end at the beginning, so we can go on forever. Begin with our living happily ever after" (*S*, p. 365).

Every romance, however, feeds on a disregard for reality, and the three participants of the story (Fenwick, Susan, the Author) know it. This is where the "twin" theme, one of *Sabbatical*'s leitmotifs, comes to bear on the story. Manfred (Fenwick's twin brother) and Miriam (Susan's twin sister), expiate whatever guilt the undisturbed – "unrealistic" – happiness of Fenwick and Susan creates in the Author. Manfred – like CIA nuclear weapons expert John Arthur Paisley –

disappears while on a cruise on Chesapeake Bay. Miriam, raped by a motor-cycle gang, then by her rescuer, and finally by a pickup truck driver, is later tortured by "Savak." Compared with the parallel but inverted story of Manfred and Miriam, the romance of Fenwick and Susan appears to be at best precarious. Precariousness, however, has always been the main condition of Barth's heroes. And the heroic parallels quoted in *Sabbatical* substantiate this claim. Fenwick is likened to Virgil's Aeneas, who meets Dido in the interval between being the representative of Troy's past glory and of Rome's future glory. And Susan is afraid that she might indeed be Fenwick's Dido instead of his Lavinia. Here, legend threatens to overtake life, for Barth believes that "our very homely, far-from-heroic personal experiences – simply because they are human experiences – contain the general pattern and connect with the great myths."[15]

Supra-realism is a parody of realism; yet parody here only means that mimesis, the imitation of life, is superseded by the attempt to turn narration into life, life into a story. The thematic importance of "forks and confluences" throughout the novel confirms this notion. It finds emblematic expression in the vignette on the title-page of the book: a circle divided into three equal wedges, forming a Y, whose center is occupied by another circle. The inner circle has a double meaning. It represents, first, the egg which, after coming down one of the two Fallopian tubes, is met by the sperm coming up the vagina. Second, it means the story as substitute for the child which would have been the outcome of the conjunction of egg and sperm, since the narrative point of view is the conjoined view of Fenwick and Susan (the story seen from the vantage point of "we") plus the semi-omniscient view of the Author ("what we can't do as Fenn and Susan, we can do as Author" (*S*, p. 135). Together the three (like the three equal wedges) define the present position of the protagonists as a confluence of their past and their future, thus establishing a cyclical – circular – pattern.

6

CONCLUSION:
THE SENSE OF A BEGINNING

The fiction of John Barth is structured on the principle of paradox or, as Barth himself would put it, having it both ways. These paradoxes can be of a logical, historical, or existential nature. Yet underlying every variant is a basic paradox, one that becomes visible only when seen in the context of the whole of the author's fictional life – a paradox moreover, which would initially not be more evident to Barth himself than to his reader and critic. The recurring feature of Barth's fiction is his concentration, each time in a pair of complementary novels, on a particular genre, which, through parody, he takes toward a *reductio ad absurdum* while at the same time reaffirming the historical presuppositions of genres as such. The hidden paradox, then, derives less from the tension between those two novels than from that between the authorial impulse for innovation and a given body of literary texts. Although the author in each case has the pair of complementary novels exhaust certain generic possibilities from two opposite poles – as if to leave the genre without any escape from his attack – the true paradox consists in the ultimate disrespect the ironic author has to exhibit toward the very tradition that sustains him. Barth's generic novels are designed to be the last of their kind – in order that beyond them new vistas may open up for literature. In other words, what makes Barth's treatment of literature, as exemplified by the sequence of his fictions, paradoxical is the fact that his own literary career continues to undermine the sense of an ending created in each pair of complementary novels. For him, traditional art and personal life enter into a dialectical relationship centering in the figure of the Author. Like the Roman god Janus, Barth faces both ways: toward reality and toward fiction, problematizing and at the same time reconciling their ontological separateness through his double, or ironic, point of view. This is why Barth may be called one of the quintessential authors of what has come to be seen as postmodernism in literature.

The paradox of postmodernism is evident in the term itself. It is both offshoot of and revolt against modernism; it acknowledges modernism's influence and power while questioning its contemporary appropriateness. Postmodernism derives from a sense of an ending, the passing of a major literary movement into history; and also from a sense of a beginning, the contemporary potential of new conditions and ways of story-telling. It assigns modernism to the historical past, making it a pre-text, something which may only be quoted; but, asserting the influence of that past, it also proposes that modernist texts remain usable in the process of constituting an art for the future. For Barth this situation is more than an academic problem or an aesthetic conceit. Though he is a learned and allusive writer, writing postmodernist fictions, for him, becomes a rebellious and heartfelt paradoxical re-enactment of the father/son relationship. The pre-modernist writers used to employ the romantic cliché that the poet uses his heart's blood as ink. One familiar comic trope in Barth's fictions is the replacement of this cliché by a postmodernist metaphoric view of the relation between the pen and the penis — mirroring and at the same time transcending the revolt of modernism against tradition, especially the tradition of Romanticism. Although introduced in parodic fashion, the implied analogy is more than a pun. The author is a creator, engendering something on something else. Fictions are begotten, and, like children, they then become independent of their author. The processes of conception and gestation are, therefore, of central importance, since it is only during these periods that the lives of the creator and his creation overlap. In Barth's story "Night-Sea Journey," a sperm swims toward a conception which turns on the pun that it may be "the talebearer of a generation" (LF, p. 9).

Barth's fictions test the concept of authorship in its form as authoritative fatherhood, and the protean and chimeric qualities of the Author are crucial to Barth's own sense of being a literary descendant. It is only if the author does *not* write with his heart's blood, does not extinguish himself in the act of creation, and retains the freedom to move onward into a new role and a new stage of literary life that the monumentalism of the writers who went before can be avoided. However, even one's own previous fictional characters can unite to pose the same threat. They can grow large enough to challenge their progenitor, subtracting from the existence of the author and making him a participant in the world of his own writing. "If only roads *did* end," complains Jacob Horner, protagonist of *The End of the Road* and summoned back again in *LETTERS*, "but the end of one is the commencement of another, or its mere continuation" (*L*, p. 279). Yet Barth once more regains his freedom by making his own ambiguous role of author the true narrative. He re-enacts himself as Author with a capital A, that is, as a character in his own fiction – in order to salvage for himself his further role of author or Author's double.

The capital-A author is the ultimate hero of Barth's fiction. As a first step toward his conception, one can see the author's creation of his own fictional *alter ego* with Ambrose in *Lost in the Funhouse*. In "Ambrose His Mark," "Water-Message," and "Lost in the Funhouse," Ambrose – not yet called "Ambrose Mensch" as he is in *LETTERS*[16] – clearly resembles John Barth. Both were born in 1930; both live in Dorchester County, Maryland; both are myopic, and this leads them both to neglect the visible world in order to "see" the truth of the invisible world of the imagination. And both Ambrose and Barth decide to become writers. However, living at one and the same time, as it were, the author John Barth could never overcome the ontological barrier that separated him from his *alter ego* Ambrose. He had to continue to be a citizen of reality and live within its limits, whereas his fictional *alter ego* was potentially free – yet tied to the conditions of the author's own life. In other words, the relationship between ego and *alter ego* did not serve to liberate the ego, it rather retained the *alter ego* within the boundaries defined by the ego's limited range of possibilities. The concept of *alter ego* undoubtedly represented an advance in self-reflexion over the heroes of Barth's first novels, who simply presented models of identification (in the figure of the protagonist) or role models (in the figure of the antagonist). Nevertheless, the concept of contemporaneous *alter ego* did not ultimately provide sufficient imaginative freedom for the author.

Whereas the real mode of existence of John Barth, as opposed to the fictional one of Ambrose Mensch, could not be changed, their contemporaneity could. Barth could envision his *alter ego* as having lived in the past or as living in the future. In this case the present-day author could either see himself as re-enacting what a former-day *alter ego* had once enacted, or he could see himself as enacting what a latter-day *alter ego* would re-enact. This device proved to be more than a camouflage; it opened up new literary passageways. As a possible authentic figure from the past or the future, the mythic hero came to Barth's mind, since, as Lord Raglan has pointed out,[17] all traditionally known mythic heroes follow the same course: from extraordinary conception and virgin birth to a stage of departure, followed by a stage of initiation, peaking in a sacred marriage; then follow the stages of return and reign, culminating in an extraordinary death, usually on a hilltop. Moreover, not only do all mythic heroes live according to this repeated pattern, but the pattern only becomes obvious in the course of historical time, or more to the author's point, by being told and retold, again and again, in the course of time. And in the end the pattern becomes more important than any proof that the mythic hero who fulfills it did in fact exist. This predominance of fiction, of narrative repetition over life, became the starting-point for Barth's development of a concept of *alter ego* who, like a mythic hero, is removed from the author in time. The author's very belatedness or precedence thus admitted him access to new narrative possibilities, replacing mere repetition – which defies time – with repetition *in time* – which, like parody, may erode the form as well as the content of the literary model it repeats. By fictionalizing this concept in the second part of *Lost in the Funhouse* as well as in *Chimera*, Barth created a realm of imaginative freedom – as opposed to the *alter ego*'s former confinement within the existential boundaries of the author's life.

The second part of *Lost in the Funhouse*, especially, appears as a *tour de force* of the imagination in which the author abandons the "real" *alter ego* for a mythic one, at the same time creating a parody of Joyce's "realistic" *Portrait of the Artist as a Young Man*. As *Lost in the Funhouse* progresses, it recedes in historical time; consequently, the *alter ego* of the author fades (it can no longer be "seen") while the narrative voice of the – as yet implied – Author gains strength. It finally becomes the voice of the anonymous mythical minstrel, mentioned in passing by Homer in the *Odyssey*. What this minstrel has set down in writing (since he is marooned on a lonely island, his writing *is* his narrative voice) has been repeated or re-enacted through the millennia of recorded time, for what he created are all the known literary genres. They are to be repeated, or re-enacted, one last time by one John Barth. That literary genres were created at some point in the past does not presuppose real creators (whose lives might be chronicled by literary historians); it only presupposes an unseen – or mythical – first instance. Thus, the narrative voice can become anonymous without denying its source. The transcendence of the ontological barrier between real author and mythic *alter ego* is represented by the dissolution, in story-telling, of the distinction between historical identity and mythic anonymity.

This is the reason for Barth's unflagging interest in story-telling: it can make the author into an Author. Understanding, also, that the Author's independent attitude was the result of his, the author's, liberation from the limitations of historical identity, Barth began to wonder whether the Author's imaginative freedom could not be reapplied to reality. The advantages of such a return must have seemed obvious: instead of having to relate exclusively to an imaginary past or future, the Author could reconnect with the author and thus with contemporary life, and he could do it on his own terms. The difference, in other words, lies in who dictates the rules of the game: life or fiction. At this point, that is when he began to write *LETTERS*, Barth had already created his own tradition of literature via literary texts which had become a reality in the world. These texts, moreover, by parodying a number of important literary genres, were consciously related to western literary tradition as such. Thus Barth could rely on a common as well as on a self-established heritage when he returned to reality. He had, of course, to be careful which areas of reality he chose, and take care to exorcise any possibility of chance alternatives which might disrupt his game. Yet the odds seemed to him, if not negligible, then at least manageable.

What makes Barth a central figure of the postmodernist literary movement, then, is this transmutation of exhausted literary genres into a sequence of so many fictionalized existential experiences which, like life itself as long as it lasts, can never be exhausted. In regarding the relationship between literary modernism and postmodernism as one of paternal lineage, Barth's literary development brings postmodernist fiction to life. The fact that Barth has chosen parody as his favored mode of writing signifies that he accepts his literary predecessors as models and yet rejects their fictions as artifacts. Parody for him mirrors the father/son conflict. Other postmodernist writers (like Donald Barthelme, Robert Coover, William Gaddis, or William Gass) have relied more heavily on experimental techniques in order to convey their postmodernist point of view. Some of those techniques Barth has helped to define, most notably in *Lost in the Funhouse*; yet he is more important in the sense that no other postmodernist writer has internalized the conflict between tradition and the self to the same degree. This conflict informs Barth's whole life – the real as well as the literary.

On with the life-story.

NOTES

1 See Nathaniel Hawthorne, *The House of the Seven Gables*, Centenary Edition, 2 (Columbus, 1965), p. 1.
2 John Barth, "The Literature of Exhaustion," *Atlantic Monthly*, 220, 1967; reprinted in John Barth, *The Friday Book: Essays and Other Nonfiction* (New York, 1984), pp. 64–76; "The Literature of Replenishment: Postmodernist Fiction," *The Atlantic*, 245, 1980; reprinted in Barth, *The Friday Book*, pp. 194–206.
3 See John Barth, "How to Make a Universe," *The Friday Book*, pp. 13–25.
4 Edward H. Cohen, *Ebenezer Cooke: The Sot-Weed Canon* (Athens, Ga., 1975).
5 See Alan Holder, "'What Marvellous Plot ... Was Afoot?' History in Barth's *The Sot-Weed Factor*," *American Quarterly*, 20, 1968, pp. 596–604; John M. Bradbury, "Absurd Insurrection: The Barth-Percy Affair," *The South Atlantic Quarterly*, 68, 1969, pp. 319–29.
6 See my interview with John Barth in Heide Ziegler and Christopher Bigsby (eds), *The Radical Imagination and the Liberal Tradition: Interviews with English and American Novelists* (London, 1982), p. 19.
7 See Evelyn Glaser-Wöhrer's second interview with John Barth in Evelyn Glaser-Wöhrer, *An Analysis of John Barth's "Weltanschauung": His View of Life and Literature*, Salzburger Studien zur Anglistik und Amerikanistik, 5 (Salzburg, 1977), p. 252.
8 In Barth's original manuscript of *Lost in the Funhouse*, deposited in the Library of Congress, the order of the two sections was "correct," the section "Lake Erie" preceding "Niagara Falls."
9 Barth had originally intended to place the "Dunyazadiad" at the end of the book instead of the beginning. See David Morrell, *John Barth: An Introduction* (University Park, Pa. and London, 1976), pp. 162–3. The inherent logic of the narratives would argue for this first choice. Not only would it have placed the "Bellerophoniad," the central story of the book, at its center, but it would also

have enabled the author to end *Chimera* on a note of qualified hope ("Good morning, then! Good morning!" (*CH*, p. 63)), developing from a note of qualified despair at the beginning of the book ("Good evening." (*CH*, p. 67)). This beginning would have been identical with the beginning of the "Perseid" which is supposedly repeated each night, after the constellation of Perseus and Medusa rises above the horizon. However, it is also told at night because it compares to the stories of *The Thousand and One Nights*. At first glance this fact seems to undermine the above argument (or plea for a reconsideration by the author of the arrangement of the novellas in a future edition), since the reader might be said to associate the "Perseid" with the Arabian stories only *after* having read the "Dunyazadiad." However, the parallel is already evoked by the title, "Dunyazadiad," as is the notion of the threat presented by the break of day, when constellations disappear and when Scheherazade must tremble for her life once more. Indeed, this threat is evoked only if the reader as yet knows nothing but the title of the "Dunyazadiad," since the novella itself presents the threat as tempered by the fact that The Genie can assure Scheherazade from the very beginning that her device to beguile the King with stories will succeed. Therefore, *Chimera* ought to end with Dunyazade's (and Barth's) acceptance of the "Tragic View of Storytelling" that will still allow, and indeed demand, the telling of another story.

10 Brian Stonehill argues that Barth's fictional characters seem more like real people in *LETTERS* because they are no longer "contained between the covers of a single book." See Brian Stonehill, "A Trestle of Letters," *Fiction International*, 12, 1980, p. 261.

11 The attitude Barth was implicitly trying to debunk was first and foremost represented by John Gardner, whose attack on postmodernist fiction, *On Moral Fiction* (New York, 1978) was published one year before *LETTERS* came out.

12 See James Joyce, *Ulysses* (Harmondsworth, 1969), pp. 31, 40.

13 Here Barth exploits a familiar American cliché: the belated attempt by many Americans to dissociate themselves from the whites' behavior to the Indians on the basis of a claim to a part Indian heritage. As Vine Deloria, Jr., points out, this claim is characteristically for an Indian grandmother who is also a princess. See Vine Deloria, Jr., *Custer Died for Your Sins: An Indian Manifesto* (New York, 1970), p. 11.

14 See Curt Suplee's interview with John Barth, "The Barth Factor," *International Herald Tribune*, 24 June 1982, p. 14.

15 ibid.

16 In *Lost in the Funhouse* Barth deleted Ambrose's surname from the final version of the stories.

17 See FitzRoy Richard Somerset Baron Raglan, *The Hero: A Study in Tradition, Myth, and Drama* (Westport, Conn., 1975), pp. 173–95.

BIBLIOGRAPHY

WORKS BY JOHN BARTH

The Floating Opera. New York: Appleton, Century Crofts, 1956. Rev. edn Garden City, NY: Doubleday, 1967. London: Secker & Warburg, 1968. New York: Bantam, 1972.

The End of the Road. Garden City, NY: Doubleday, 1958. London: Secker & Warburg, 1962. Rev. edn Garden City, NY: Doubleday, 1967. New York: Bantam, 1969.

The Sot-Weed Factor. Garden City, NY: Doubleday, 1960. London: Secker & Warburg, 1961. Rev. edn Garden City, NY: Doubleday, 1967. New York: Bantam, 1969.

Giles Goat-Boy or, The Revised New Syllabus. Garden City, NY: Doubleday, 1966. London: Secker & Warburg, 1967. Greenwich, Conn.: Fawcett Crest, 1967.

Lost in the Funhouse: Fiction for Print, Tape, Live Voice. Garden City, NY: Doubleday, 1968. London: Secker & Warburg, 1969.

"Seven Additional Author's Notes." *Lost in the Funhouse*. New York: Bantam, 1969. (Added for this edition.)

Chimera. New York: Random House, 1972. Greenwich, Conn.: Fawcett Crest, 1973. London: André Deutsch, 1974.

LETTERS. New York: Putnam, 1979. London: Secker & Warburg, 1980.

Sabbatical: A Romance. New York: Putnam, 1982. Harmondsworth: Penguin, 1983.

The Friday Book: Essays and Other Nonfiction. New York: Putnam, 1984. (A collection which includes Barth's previously published non-fiction.)

Interviews with John Barth

Bellamy, Joe David (ed.). *The New Fiction: Interviews with Innovative American Writers*, pp. 1–18. Urbana and Chicago: University of Illinois Press, 1974.

Enck, John. "John Barth: An Interview." In L. S. Dembo and Cyrena

M. Podrom (eds), *The Contemporary Writer: Interviews with Sixteen Novelists and Poets*, pp. 18–29. Madison: University of Wisconsin Press, 1972.

LeClair, Tom, and McCaffery, Larry (eds). "A Dialogue: John Barth and John Hawkes," *Anything Can Happen: Interviews with Contemporary American Novelists*, pp. 9–19. Urbana and Chicago: University of Illinois Press, 1983.

McKenzie, James (ed.). "Pole-Vaulting in Top-Hats: A Public Conversation with John Barth, William Gass, and Ishmael Reed." *Modern Fiction Studies*, 22, 2 (1976), pp. 131–51.

Reilly, Charlie. "An Interview with John Barth." *Contemporary Literature*, 22, 1 (1981), pp. 1–23.

Ziegler, Heide, and Bigsby, Christopher (eds). "John Barth," *The Radical Imagination and the Liberal Tradition: Interviews with English and American Novelists*, pp. 16–38. London: Junction Books, 1982.

Bibliography

Weixlmann, Joseph. *John Barth: A Descriptive Primary and Annotated Secondary Bibliography, Including a Descriptive Catalog of Manuscript Holdings in United States Libraries*. New York and London: Garland, 1976.

SELECTED CRITICISM OF JOHN BARTH

D'Haen, Theo. *Text to Reader: A Communicative Approach to Fowles, Barth, Cortazar and Boon*. Amsterdam: Benjamins, 1983.

Graff, Gerald. "Under Our Belt and Off Our Back: Barth's *LETTERS* and Postmodern Fiction." *TriQuarterly*, 52 (Fall 1981), pp. 150–64.

Harris, Charles B. *Passionate Virtuosity: The Fiction of John Barth*. Urbana and Chicago: University of Illinois Press, 1983.

Hauck, Richard Boyd. *A Cheerful Nihilism: Confidence and "The Absurd" in American Humorous Fiction*. Bloomington: Indiana University Press, 1971.

Hawkes, John. "*The Floating Opera* and *Second Skin*." *Mosaic*, 8, 1 (1974), pp. 17–28.

Mercer, Peter. "The Rhetoric of *Giles Goat-Boy*." *Novel*, 4, 2 (1971), pp. 147–58.

Morrell, David. *John Barth: An Introduction*. University Park: Pennsylvania State University Press, 1976.

Morris, Christopher D. "Barth and Lacan: The World of the Moebius Strip." *Critique*, 17, 1 (1975), pp. 69–77.

O'Donnell, Patrick. *Passionate Doubts: Designs of Interpretation in*

Contemporary American Fiction. Iowa City: University of Iowa Press, 1986.

Pütz, Manfred. *The Story of Identity: American Fiction of the Sixties*. Amerikastudien/American Studies, 54. Stuttgart: Metzler, 1979.

Robins, Deborah J. "Whatever Happened to Realism: John Barth's *LETTERS*." *Northwest Review*, 19, 1/2 (1981), pp. 218–27.

Scholes, Robert. *Fabulation and Metaficton*. Urbana and Chicago: University of Illinois Press, 1979.

Schulz, Max F. *Black Humor Fiction of the Sixties: A Pluralistic Definition of Man and His World*. Athens: Ohio University Press, 1973.

—— "Barth, *LETTERS*, and the Great Tradition." *Genre*, 14, 1 (1981), pp. 95–115.

Stark, John. *The Literature of Exhaustion: Borges, Nabokov and Barth*. Durham: Duke University Press, 1974.

Stonehill, Brian. "A Trestle of Letters." *Fiction International*, 12 (1980), pp. 259–68.

Tanner, Tony. *City of Words: American Fiction, 1950–1970*. New York: Harper & Row, 1971.

—— "Games American Writers Play. Ceremony, Complicity, Contestation, and Carnival." *Salmagundi*, 34 (Fall 1976), pp. 121–9.

Tharpe, Jac. *John Barth: The Comic Sublimity of Paradox*. With a preface by Harry T. Moore. Carbondale: Southern Illinois University Press; London: Feffer & Simons, 1974.

Vintanza, Victor J. "The Novelist as Topologist: John Barth's *Lost in the Funhouse*." *Texas Studies in Language and Literature*, 19, 1 (1977), pp. 83–97.

Waldmeir, Joseph J. (ed.) *Critical Essays on John Barth*. Boston: Hall, 1980. (This collection gathers together the most important essays on John Barth's fiction through 1979.)